W9-BDZ-193

The Sino-Soviet Confrontation: Implications for The Future

DK 68.7
C 5
H 56

NOV 24 1981

212244

The Sino-Soviet Confrontation: *Implications for The Future*

Harold C. Hinton

PUBLISHED BY

Crane, Russak & Company, Inc.

NEW YORK

National Strategy
Information Center, Inc.

The Sino-Soviet Confrontation:
Implications for the Future

Published in the United States by
Crane, Russak & Company, Inc.
347 Madison Avenue
New York, N.Y. 10017

Copyright © 1976 National Strategy Information Center, Inc.
111 East 58th Street
New York, N.Y. 10022

No part of this publication may be reproduced,
stored in a retrieval system, or transmitted
in any form or by any means, electronic,
mechanical, photocopying, recording,
or otherwise, without the prior
written permission of the publisher.

Library Edition: ISBN 0-8448-1048-7
Paperbound Edition: ISBN 0-8448-1049-5
LC 76-47857

Strategy Paper No. 29

Printed in the United States of America

Table of Contents

Preface

The Communist takeover of mainland China in 1949 was one of the watershed developments of contemporary history. A new Communist colossus now took its place beside the Soviet Union in the permanent struggle against the democratic, capitalist West. Perhaps equally significant in its implications for international affairs, and generally less expected, was the emergence of overt rivalry and conflict between China and the Soviet Union in the 1960s, after a brief period of alliance and close collaboration. More than anything else, this development has undermined the initial bipolar structure of post-World War II politics, and initiated a period of much greater fluidity and uncertainty in relations among the great powers. For the United States in particular, the Sino-Soviet dispute seemed to offer substantial opportunities for maneuver, and certainly posed difficult policy choices with respect to both Communist superpowers.

The death of Mao Tse-tung affords a convenient moment to reappraise the ongoing conflict between Russia and China, and to reassess its implications for United States policy. Professor Hinton's essay was completed just before Mao's passing, and addresses itself to the many problems and uncertainties which that event will inevitably sharpen. After sketching the early evolution of the Sino-Soviet dispute, Hinton analyzes in detail the main issues involved, and how the two sides have sought to deal with the situation, and where possible to take advantage of it. Special attention is also given to the American response, and to the Nixon-Kissinger-Ford initiatives toward detente with both Russia and China after 1969.

With respect to the future course of the dispute, Hinton's general conclusion is that a "full-fledged Sino-Soviet rapprochement or reconciliation is not likely," although some amelioration of present tensions is entirely possible. In this connection, much will depend on the outcome of the struggle for succession to Mao's mantle. As for the United States, we have "benefited" from the dispute, although "without having caused it or having been able actively to exploit it." This situation is unlikely to change very much over the foreseeable future.

Professor Harold C. Hinton is one of this country's leading authorities on Chinese politics and Sino-Soviet Relations. He was educated at Harvard University, from which he received his Ph.D. in 1951; and is now Professor of Political Science and International Affairs at George Washington University. Among his most recent books are *The Bear at the Gate: Chinese Policymaking Under Soviet Pressure* (1971), *An Introduction to Chinese Politics* (1973), and *Three and a Half Powers: The New Balance in Asia* (1975).

Frank R. Barnett, *President*
National Strategy Information Center, Inc.

September 1976

1

Introduction

When it burst upon the world in the early 1960s, the Sino-Soviet dispute was a sensation to Communists and non-Communists alike. If it is no longer a sensation, this is because it has become familiar, not because it has ceased to be important. Indeed, the dispute has escalated to the level of a military confrontation that today appears to hold the only serious likelihood of war between two major powers. To be sure, the prospect of war seems to have receded since 1969; but the danger is still there, and its consequences would be catastrophic, not only for the belligerents, but also for the stability of Asia and for American interests in East Asia.

The absence of spectacular recent developments—apart from events surrounding the 1969 border crisis—is not the only reason for the decline of general interest in the Sino-Soviet dispute since the early 1960s. Another is the obscurity of many aspects of the dispute, and in particular of the language and other means by which the two sides communicate with, denounce, and maneuver against each other. But such obscurity does not diminish the importance of the subject, which as in other fields can be made to yield to systematic analysis.

This study is intended to clear up the obscurity, to the extent that this can be done on the basis of the public record. It analyzes briefly the origins and causes of the Sino-Soviet dispute, and attempts to explain the border crisis of 1969, which raised the dispute to the level of a dangerous military confrontation, and its aftermath. The possible future development of the Sino-Soviet relationship is discussed in detail.

1

While all options remain open, the two most extreme—war and a full reconciliation—appear the least likely to materialize.

To what extent is it possible to analyze this complex subject on the basis of the public record? The answer is that, after the experience of two decades reaching back into the period when Sino-Soviet relations were much more friendly, it is possible to do a great deal along these lines. Content analysis of statements emanating from Moscow and Peking, comparison of the views of other students of the Sino-Soviet relationship, and—above all—consideration of the historical record of what the two adversaries have actually done, can yield impressive results. Off-the-record discussions with officials of both sides—the Soviets are more forthcoming in this respect than the Chinese—can be interesting, but must be treated with great caution. Moscow has been trying with some success in recent years to influence American opinion in a variety of ways, including invitations to American China-watchers to visit the Soviet Union. In general, the accompanying Soviet "revelations" are highly unreliable. More recently, Peking's liaison staff in the United States has taken to holding "conversations" with American Soviet-watchers, presumably both to learn from them and to influence their views.

2

Origins and Issues of the
Sino-Soviet Dispute

Recent developments in the Communist countries have made it clear that national political traditions and old international rivalries are still important. From that perspective, the Sino-Soviet relationship has a long and predominantly unfavorable history.

The Past

On the Soviet side, the Russians tend to harbor a racial dislike of Chinese at least as great as what they feel for other Asians, including Soviet Asians. The Chinese appear as not only the most numerous, but as currently the most dangerous, of a long line of Asian threats stretching back through the Japanese Empire to the Central Asian nomads of the Middle Ages. This threat has seemed most serious when it appeared to coincide with a threat from the west, usually from the direction of Germany. Such a two-front danger actually obtained during the period of the German-Japanese axis, and to a much lesser extent —in fact, mainly in Soviet propaganda alleging the existence of a "Bonn-Peking axis"—from 1966 to 1968, when China was convulsed by the Cultural Revolution, which had strong anti-Soviet overtones, and West Germany was trying to isolate East Germany through the first version of its *Ostpolitik*. This inherited fear and dislike of the Chinese has been aggravated by the robotlike discipline and work habits of Chinese students and technicians who came to the Soviet

3

Union after 1949. So detested are the Chinese that, as one acute observer has said, only half jokingly, next to lowering the price of vodka nothing would increase the popularity of the Soviet regime more than declaring war on China.

On the Chinese side, Russia—unlike China's other modern adversaries—has encroached on China by land, and therefore stands in a sense as the successor of the Central Asian nomads who once ravaged China as well as Russia. Tsarist Russia inflicted territorial losses and military defeats on China second only to those imposed by Japan. At other times, Russia posed as China's friend and protector against the other powers in order to extract unilateral advantages for itself; to a considerable extent, and with some justification, this is the way the Chinese have come to view Soviet policy toward China, both from 1917 to 1949 and since 1949. This attitude had much to do with the resentment and hostility that Soviet technicians encountered in China even in the early years after 1949.

Political and Ideological Differences

For a variety of reasons, the political systems of the two adversaries have developed along very different lines under the common label of Marxism-Leninism. Each reflects to a great extent the political tradition of its own people. The Soviet system remains Stalinist to a considerable degree; it is bureaucratically administered by the Communist Party apparatus, with the powerful assistance of a huge secret police network (the KGB), and it still expects deference from foreign Communist Parties. The Chinese, even before the Cultural Revolution, have placed less emphasis on bureaucratic and police controls and more on propaganda and social organization legitimated with the name and "thought" of Mao Tse-tung. Because the Soviet system, for historical reasons, has acquired the aura of Marxist-Leninist orthodoxy, the Chinese have been "unorthodox" in Soviet eyes ever since the distinctive features of their system began to emerge clearly after the mid-1950s.

As long as Stalin lived, Mao acknowledged himself as junior, although he would not allow China to become a Soviet satellite. But with Stalin's death in 1953, Mao came to regard himself as senior and superior to Stalin's quarreling successors. In 1956, the clumsiness of Khrushchev's attack on Stalin's memory and of his handling of the crises in Poland and Hungary led Mao to begin offering independent ideological and political guidance to the international Communist movement, including the Soviet Communist Party itself. By about 1959, Mao had come to consider Khrushchev as much of a "revisionist" as Tito—or, in other words, soft in his domestic policies and insufficiently militant in confronting American "imperialism" around the world. Since the fundamentalist Communist leadership of Albania agreed with Peking that Khrushchev was "revisionist," China and Albania became close friends after 1960, much to Moscow's annoyance. Khrushchev, although not very ideologically inclined, resented Mao's attacks on Soviet policies and Mao's increasingly explicit claim to unique ideological correctness and authority within the international Communist movement. After 1960, the rival ideologies, claims to authority, and policy positions of the two contestants did not so much create a clear split within the movement as accelerate a general decentralizing trend that had begun with the Stalin-Tito controversy in 1948. Moscow was no longer the unchallenged center, but neither was Peking. After Khrushchev's fall in 1964, Mao's personal and ideological pretensions continued to grow and culminated during the Cultural Revolution of 1966-68, one of whose main purposes was to eliminate any possibility of "revisionist," Soviet-style communism gaining control of China, even after Mao's death. The reaction of Khrushchev's successors to Mao's performance was no more favorable, although it was somewhat less emotional, than Khrushchev's had been.

Coping with the United States

Nothing contributed more to the emergence and growth of the Sino-Soviet dispute than their different relationships with and policies toward the United States. Mao persuaded Stalin in February 1950 to give him an alliance against the supposedly aggressive United States and a possibly resurgent Japan. Under this umbrella, China managed to fight the United States in Korea without becoming the target of American retaliation. But as the Korean War began, so did another issue that was to impose an enormous strain on the Sino-Soviet relationship: Taiwan. To Peking, Taiwan was (and is) Chinese territory; and its consistent insistence that the extension of American protection to Taiwan on June 27, 1950, constituted "occupation" of the island was, among other things, a challenge to the Soviet Union to take some sort of responsive action as required by the Sino-Soviet alliance. Chinese pressures of this kind increased after the Korean War and then the

First Indochina War came to an end (the latter in July 1954), and after the United States had negotiated a mutual security treaty with Taiwan at the end of 1954. Peking apparently wanted Moscow to give some sort of support for the "liberation" of Taiwan, or at least to put pressure on the United States somewhere else—West Berlin, in all probability. But to Moscow, the Taiwan issue was not worth a confrontation with the United States; and the Soviets claimed that Peking was trying to pervert the Sino-Soviet alliance from defense to offense.

The huge advantage held by the United States over the Soviet Union in nuclear and thermonuclear warheads and delivery systems for a decade after the mid-1950s increased Soviet reluctance to take risky actions on China's behalf. To Mao and his more militant colleagues, this was a betrayal of China and the appeasement of "imperialism." He insisted that reverse brinkmanship by the Soviet Union could force a supposedly irresolute American "paper tiger" out of such positions as West Berlin and, above all, Taiwan without a major war, because the "Socialist camp" was superior to the "imperialist camp," if not in strategic weapons, then in the overall "correlation of forces" (that is the balance of all psychological, political, economic, military, and other factors). Again Khrushchev disagreed, or at any rate did not feel willing to gamble on Mao being right. The most he agreed to do under Chinese pressure, and it was a great deal, was to initiate a program of military nuclear assistance to China in 1957—only to terminate it in 1959, when Peking's assertiveness began to worry him and to endanger his relations with the United States and India. Khrushchev's Cuban missile ploy of 1962 was probably undertaken under pressure from colleagues less anti-Chinese than he, and partly in the hope of improving relations with the Chinese by pressuring the United States to withdraw its protection of Taiwan. When he failed, he launched a policy of detente with the United States, of which the Limited Nuclear Test Ban Treaty of 1963 was the high point, and which drove Peking to furious polemics against him.

The Third World

Another major issue in the Sino-Soviet dispute, especially in the late 1950s and early 1960s, concerned the best strategy for revolutionizing and ultimately communizing the Third World. Moscow's greater strategic power made it a more likely target of American "massive retaliation" in the event of a major crisis arising in the Third

World or elsewhere. On the other hand, the Soviet self-image and its vast resources, plus Chinese pressures and demands for support from local revolutionaries, made it impossible for Moscow to opt out of the revolutionary game altogether. The problem of operating under these conditions was a difficult one for Khrushchev, and has remained difficult for his successors. In practice, the Soviet Union has tended to support, rather than try to overthrow, Third World regimes that appeared to be fairly well established and were at least somewhat leftist and anti-American, unless they were also strongly pro-Chinese. India is probably the most important example of such a state.

Peking's problem was somewhat simpler. Having a fairly clearly defined revolutionary doctrine (in essence, guerrilla or "people's" war) for Third World countries based on its own experience, and less concerned over possible American retaliation so long as a crisis did not arise on China's immediate periphery, with fewer resources and less responsibility in the eyes of the international left, Peking could and did preach a policy of militant, "self-reliant" struggle against actual or alleged "imperialist" influence in the Third World. It also provided limited amounts of aid to such struggles, and condemned the Soviet approach—and some Third World governments supported by Moscow —as reactionary. This was especially true of India, which furthermore was a rival of Peking in Asia and the Third World generally, and which also had a serious border dispute with China.

The Sino-Soviet controversy over the Third World remained somewhat academic, although it was seriously intended. There were few opportunities for a comparative test of the Soviet and Chinese approaches; and, in fact, neither was fully relevant to the problem. On the whole, Third World governments went their own way, picking and choosing as they saw fit from the examples, advice, aid, and support offered by Moscow, Peking, and other sources.

The Dispute Surfaces

By about 1960, Mao had decided that Soviet ideology and foreign policy were so inimical to the interests of China and communism as he interpreted them that they deserved treatment as an adversary. Soviet "revisionism" entered the Maoist demonology as an enemy roughly as detestable as American "imperialism," although not (yet) militarily so dangerous to China.

The issues (that is, Soviet "revisionism" versus Chinese "dogmatism") were thrashed out, vigorously but inconclusively, in a series of meetings and published polemics that began in the Spring of 1960 and peaked in 1963-64, shortly before Khrushchev's fall from power in October 1964.

Vietnam

Khrushchev's successors evidently believed that he had overreacted to his controversy with the Chinese. They accordingly offered Peking an accommodation involving a suspension of ideological polemics, a resumption of normal trade and Soviet aid, and, above all, "united action" over Vietnam, where the war escalated abruptly in early 1965. It is possible that some of Mao's colleagues were interested in this offer, but Mao himself wanted no part of it. He was convinced, especially after Moscow in March 1965 revived Khrushchev's plan for an international conference of Communist Parties, which was known to be unacceptable to Mao, that the Brezhnev-Kosygin leadership was at least as "revisionist" as Khrushchev. With some reason, Mao saw the proposal for "united action" as a Soviet device for assuming leadership of the Communist struggle against American "imperialism" in Vietnam. The most that could be salvaged by Moscow under these conditions was an agreement for the movement of Soviet military equipment to North Vietnam across the already badly overloaded Chinese rail system. Mao and his supporters, notably Defense Minister Lin Piao, concluded that the struggle in Vietnam should be carried on in as "self-reliant" a manner as possible, or in other words with the least possible aid and interference from China and others; and that "united action" was neither required by a sufficient American threat to China itself, nor permissible in view of the "revisionist" nature of the Soviet leadership.

In fact, Soviet and Chinese policies toward the Vietnam War were competitive and almost hostile, subject to the limitation that neither wanted to antagonize Hanoi unduly by appearing more deeply committed to the Sino-Soviet dispute than to Hanoi's struggle against American "imperialism." Each side denounced the other as a traitor to the cause of the Vietnamese "people" (that is, Hanoi and the Viet Cong). Soviet sources accused the Chinese of deliberately disrupting the flow of materiel to Vietnam by rail; it is probable that there were some delays, but more likely on account of the Cultural Revolution than for any other reason. But whether by land or by sea, enough

Soviet materiel reached North Vietnam to have an ultimately decisive effect on the struggle. Moscow urged Hanoi—behind the scenes, so as not to appear to be giving aid and comfort to the United States—to seek a negotiated settlement of the conflict, on the ground that it would bring a political victory even more surely than the use of force, and at the same time would be far less risky and costly.

Peking, on the other hand, tended to "fight to the last Vietnamese" by urging Hanoi to wage a protracted "people's war" in the Chinese manner, to avoid escalation to the level of conventional war, and to refuse negotiations. Apart from advice, propaganda, and other forms of logistical support, Peking confined its role in the war essentially to shipments of infantry weapons. One reason for this was that it did not want to risk a clash with the United States. Since Washington felt the same way, it avoided actions likely to be provocative to Peking, such as an invasion of North Vietnam. Meanwhile, the latter went its own way without paying much attention to the views of either of its giant allies. Hanoi was confident that they would not desert it so long as they did not begin to fight each other, and so long as North Vietnam did not side wholly with either in the Sino-Soviet dispute.

The Cultural Revolution

To Brezhnev and many of his colleagues, who were dedicated to the principle that a country calling itself Socialist (in the Marxist-Leninist sense, that is, Communist) ought to be led and administered by its Communist Party apparatus, the Cultural Revolution came as probably the greatest shock to the Sino-Soviet relationship to date. The shock was all the greater because it came on the heels of a rude rejection by Peking, in March 1966, of a Soviet invitation to send an observer delegation to the forthcoming 23rd Congress of the Communist Party of the Soviet Union. Such delegations were a normal courtesy among Communist Parties; and Peking gave as the reason for its refusal the recent circulation to some European Communist Parties of a Soviet "secret letter" restating Moscow's case against Peking.

The most conspicuous feature of the Cultural Revolution, apart from the rampages of the Red Guards, was the temporary overthrow of the Party apparatus by the Maoist students—urged on, of course, by Mao himself. From Moscow's point of view, this was not only a bad thing for China but a potentially harmful example for the rest of the Communist world. Moreover, during the Cultural Revolution anti-Soviet feeling in China rose to the greatest heights yet attained. For example, the Soviet Embassy in Peking was surrounded by hostile Red Guards for about two weeks in January-February 1967. There are reasons for believing that Moscow was so enraged by the Cultural Revolution that it might have staged some sort of military intervention in 1966 if any effective anti-Maoist coalition had emerged in China with which it could have cooperated; but the headlong speed of the Cultural Revolution left no time for the development of such a force. The Soviet Union was also alarmed by the Chinese Army's takeover of power in the provinces in 1967, nominally in support of the Cultural Revolution. Like the Red Guard phenomenon, this was a marked departure from the "orthodox" (that is, Soviet) way in which Communist countries were supposed to be run, and a potentially bad example for other countries. Moscow's mood was not notably improved by the Army's suppression of the Red Guards in late 1968 and the effective end of the Cultural Revolution about the same time. Soviet propaganda continued to assert, with at least some seriousness but only limited accuracy, that China was controlled by a Maoist-military-bureaucratic coalition dedicated to "expansion" at the expense of the Soviet Union and other countries.

3

The Border Crisis

Serious though the issues described in the previous chapter were, they were not sufficient to produce a military confrontation between the two parties. For that, a border dispute and a mutual perception of threat were necessary. On the Soviet side, concern began to rise in 1959, when Peking repudiated the Indian version of the eastern sector of the Sino-Indian border on the ground that it had been fixed by British "imperialism." The Sino-Soviet border obviously rested on the same foundation, except that the "imperialism" had been Tsarist Russia's.

Emergence of the Border Dispute

In 1963-64, when Peking was still fuming over the Soviet performance in the Cuban missile crisis and during the 1962 Sino-Indian border war, and also over Moscow's signing of the Test Ban Treaty, Chinese statements began to mention, for the first time in public, a fact that any one with even the most elementary knowledge of Far Eastern history knows. This was that Tsarist Russia had annexed large tracts of territory in the Far East (the Maritime Province and the northern half of the Amur watershed) and in Central Asia (portions of the Kazakh, Kirghiz, and Tadzhik Republics) that were claimed by the Manchu Empire, and that the Soviet Union had made a satellite of the Mongolian People's Republic (Outer Mongolia to the Chinese), which had been a dependency of the Manchus and, after their fall in 1912, had been claimed by the Republic of China. Chinese Communist sources, including Mao himself, asserted that the treaties (of 1858, 1860, and

11

1881) by which Tsarist Russia had compelled the Manchus to recognize these annexations were "unequal" because they had been imposed by force, and therefore theoretically invalid. The case of the Mongolian People's Republic was more difficult and was handled more carefully, since it had been granted diplomatic recognition by Peking in 1949. But there could be little doubt that, at a minimum, Peking hoped to see Chinese influence replace Soviet paramountcy.

The comparative validity of the two positions—the "inequality" of the treaties versus at least *de facto* control—is debatable; but the debate would have little meaning except as part of a political and perhaps military confrontation over the border region. That context was soon to be provided. For whether or not Peking intended its statements as anything more than propaganda, Moscow took them with great seriousness, if only because a territorial concession to China would tend to reopen the question of territorial acquisitions by Tsarist Russia and the Soviet Union elsewhere, and especially in Eastern Europe. The problem seemed all the more serious when, shortly after the militant Maoist Lin Piao became Defense Minister in 1959, parties of Chinese military personnel began to violate the border, according to numerous Soviet sources that appear credible, and enter Soviet territory before being turned back, usually with minimum force. This strange behavior was probably not so much the assertion of a territorial claim as a manifestation of contempt and defiance of Soviet "revisionism," which the Maoists considered a paper bear.

Beginnings of the Soviet Military Build-up

Paper bear or not, the Soviet Union began to reinforce its military units along the Chinese border after 1960, although not at a rapid rate. The Mongolian People's Republic was brought into Comecon (Council of Economic Mutual Assistance) in 1961, and at some later date, Moscow began trying to get it into the Warsaw Treaty Organization (or Warsaw Pact). Since Soviet influence in the Mongolian People's Republic was already overwhelming, and since the Chinese presence (economic aid programs and the like) was virtually squeezed out in the late 1950s, Moscow's motive must have been primarily security—that is, the defense of the Mongolian People's Republic against possible Chinese pressures by further legitimation of its status as a member of the Soviet camp. Similarly in early 1966, when the Cultural Revolution was about to explode and the Chinese were being difficult over Vietnam, Moscow moved combat units into the Mongolian People's Republic, probably both in order to defend it if necessary and to pose an offensive threat to Peking if that should seem desirable. At about this time, the Soviet Union also began to encourage Japanese investment in the development of the natural resources of Siberia and the Soviet Far East, probably in order to discourage Japanese support for possible Chinese claims in these areas as well as for the obvious economic reasons.

By that time, the Soviet Union had begun to regard China as a serious military threat. In 1965, Peking had begun to construct an ICBM testing range, which was a sure indication that it intended to become a thermonuclear power. In the same year, Premier Sato of Japan announced his intention to press for the reversion of Okinawa to Japanese jurisdiction, a development that would downgrade the usefulness of the island as an American base for the containment of Communist China. Moscow began to fear that the United States, preoccupied with Vietnam and likely eventually to withdraw its forces from the Western Pacific, might no longer be able to contain Chinese "expansionism" at the expense of non-Communist Asia, a possibility almost as unwelcome in Soviet eyes as the prospect of Chinese pressures on Soviet Asia.

The Cultural Revolution and Czechoslovakia

During the Cultural Revolution, the Sino-Soviet border became even more active. Red Guards and other militants staged provocative and sometimes large-scale demonstrations along the border, in addition to actual crossings. Although obviously irritated, Moscow reacted with considerable calm, probably because it realized that these incidents were manifestations of enthusiasm rather than the forerunner of serious hostilities. Local Soviet commanders were reportedly given the authority to handle such situations as they saw fit, and not much was made of the incidents by the Soviet side.

The Soviet invasion of Czechoslovakia (August 21, 1968) startled the entire Chinese leadership, and conveyed a message—although a differing one—to the two tendencies or schools within it, the Maoist "radicals" and the "moderates." The former, of whom Defense Minister Lin Piao was probably the most influential at the time, urged the Czechoslovak people to fight both the invaders and the "Dubcek revisionist clique." But they do not appear to have believed that the crisis foreshadowed a serious threat to China, or at any rate one that would require a major policy change. The moderates, led by Premier Chou En-lai, on the other hand, evidently concluded that the invasion and the ensuing proclamation of the Brezhnev Doctrine, which asserted a unilateral Soviet right to intervene in any Communist country, confirmed their view that the Soviet Union was not a paper bear, as the radicals thought, but a dangerous and unpredictable adversary whose management might require changes in Chinese policy. This impression was reinforced by a series of strongly anti-Chinese articles in Soviet theoretical journals during this period, although in fact these articles probably represented an effort by Politburo member M.A. Suslov to discourage his colleagues from invading Czechoslovakia by demonstrating that China was a much more serious problem. As early as August 23, Chou used the term "social-imperialism" to describe the new brand of Soviet behavior manifested in the invasion of Czechoslovakia, by which he meant "imperialism" (the kind of aggressive tendencies allegedly displayed by the United States) as practiced, presumably for the first time, by a country calling itself Socialist (that is, Communist).

In September, Albania committed a possibly dangerous act of defiance by announcing its withdrawal from the Soviet-dominated Warsaw Pact. Probably in order to distract Moscow's attention from Albania, as well as from Rumania and Yugoslavia, which were also feeling threatened, Peking alleged on September 16 that Soviet aircraft had recently been overflying an area of northern Manchuria. On the other hand, Albania was also given to understand, in a variety of ways, that there were limits to what Peking could do for it.

Chinese Maneuvers

It was probably in part as a precautionary measure that the Chinese Communist Party's long-planned Ninth Congress, which had already been put off a number of times, was again postponed. The timing of the Soviet invasion of Czechoslovakia had been largely determined by a desire to preempt the 14th Congress of the Czechoslovak Communist Party, scheduled for September 9; and Peking had no desire to risk having its own meeting disrupted in a similar way.

On the other hand, the Chinese had time to think and debate the alternatives. Whatever Soviet intentions might be, they evidently did not include an immediate attack on China, if only because the Winter was approaching. A Central Committee meeting in October undoubtedly discussed the problem, and may even have considered the possibility of some sort of opening to the United States. Later developments were to show, however, that whatever Mao's attitude this idea did not command the support of the radical group as a whole; and it was necessary for Chou En-lai to find ways of moving in a direction that he had evidently come to consider essential. He waited first for the results of the American Presidential election. Then on November 25, apparently after Mao had begun his Winter vacation, Chou sent a message to the United States proposing that the Sino-American ambassadorial talks at Warsaw, which had been suspended since the previous May, be resumed on February 20, 1969, by which time the incoming Nixon Administration would have had a month to get its feet on the ground. Also on November 25, he moved ingeniously to rationalize this step in the face of predictable doubts and challenges from the radicals by republishing for wide distribution a tract written by Mao in 1945, the essence of which was that at times it is permissible and even necessary to negotiate with one's adversary.

Chou also initiated what might be called a program of "deprovocation" of the Soviet Union by dismantling for a time the ICBM testing range in northwest China. Chinese sources (for example, the Sinkiang commander Yang Yung, in an interview published in the West German Socialist Party organ *Vorwärts* on November 6, 1975) have occasionally published reports to the effect that Peking's nuclear weapons production facilities have been moved from northwest China and Sinkiang to Tibet, presumably to discourage a Soviet "surgical strike" against them.

On February 19, 1969, Peking cancelled the talks scheduled at Warsaw for the following day, without indicating any interest in resuming them at a later date. The explanation given was the defection to the United States of a Chinese diplomat who subsequently returned to China. But this was almost certainly not the real reason for the cancellation, nor were some rather unfriendly remarks about Peking made by President Nixon in a press conference on January 27. The main reason was probably a shift in Peking in favor of the radical position, which was basically opposed to an opening of any kind to the United States. Mao had evidently been persuaded, probably by Lin Piao, to support cancellation of the Warsaw meeting. Mao's activities in January 1969 included a tour of the northeast (Manchuria) in the company of Lin Piao, which was a very unusual thing for the elderly Chairman, a southerner, to do during the Winter.

The 1969 Border Crisis

By the logic of the dual adversary strategy (simultaneously anti-American and anti-Soviet), which had been in effect in Peking since about 1960 and had found in Lin Piao one of its leading exponents (in his 1965 tract, *Long Live the Victory of People's War,* for example), the blow at the "imperialist" enemy represented by the cancellation of the Warsaw talks should be paralleled by some sort of blow at the "social-imperialist" enemy. Both blows would help to create, in Lin's politically naive eyes, a suitable background for convening the Ninth Party Congress, even though (or, perhaps, *because*) that would constitute a provocation of the "social-imperialists," and for his own installation at the Congress as Mao's heir to the Party leadership. There is evidence indicating that Mao and Lin scheduled the oft-postponed Ninth Party Congress for mid-March and that Lin, presumably with Mao's approval, planned his blow at the "social-imperialists" for shortly before the opening of the Congress—specifically, on the day when the Soviet Defense Minister, Marshal Grechko, was to arrive in India; real or imagined Soviet-Indian collusion against China has been something of an obsession with Peking since the late 1950s. Lin probably calculated, after late February at any rate, that a crisis that arose at that time over West Berlin would prevent the Soviet leadership, whose allergy to simultaneous crises on two fronts was well known, from retaliating for the move he was planning.

On the Soviet side, the mood along the Chinese border at that time was also tense. It is possible that Moscow was planning a move of its own, but more probably it thought that there was reason to anticipate trouble from the Chinese side. According to later statements by Peking that were not denied in Moscow, Soviet forces in mid-February went on some form of alert along the Manchurian border.

On March 2, the day of Marshal Grechko's arrival in India, Chinese forces ambushed and inflicted heavy casualties on a Soviet unit of approximately platoon strength on a frozen island (known to the Soviets as Damansky and to the Chinese as Chen Pao) in the Ussuri River, which flows between Manchuria and the Soviet Maritime Province. Each side, of course, accused the other of having provoked the incident. There is a fairly general consensus among impartial observers, however, that the initiative was Chinese—and, according to Soviet sources, specifically Lin Piao's. Moreover, there is evidence for this view in the form of a radio broadcast by the commander of a nearby Soviet unit, intercepted by at least one foreign monitoring service, in which he inquired whether it was true that another unit had been ambushed.

Peking, and probably Lin Piao in particular, were astonished and alarmed at the vigor of the Soviet reaction to this incident. Moscow promptly dropped out of the Berlin crisis and turned its attention to Peking. There was a "spontaneous" demonstration against the Chinese Embassy in Moscow, and a huge diplomatic and propaganda uproar against the Chinese "expansionists." The Soviet military, eager both to avenge their dead and to dramatize their role as defenders of the "Socialist fatherland," beat the drums about the incident in their own press, to the point apparently of perturbing their civilian colleagues; at any rate, the military component of the May Day parade was cancelled on very short notice. Moscow seized on the border tension with Peking as an issue over which to rally the Warsaw Pact countries to the standard of Soviet leadership, not only against the Chinese and in support of the vulnerable Mongolian People's Republic, but in general. This was apparently the line taken by Brezhnev at a Warsaw Pact meeting held in Budapest on March 17, when he unsuccessfully urged the inclusion of the Mongolian People's Republic in the Warsaw Pact. His line was logical in view of the declining utility of the West German bogey and Moscow's desire to complete the process of revising its bilateral treaties with the Warsaw Pact states, but it was not overly effective; Rumania in particular resented and resisted Soviet efforts to manipulate the Chinese issue to the disadvantage of the smaller Communist states.

Probably the most serious aspect of the Soviet reaction to the March 2 incident was military. On March 15, a Soviet unit of approximately battalion strength attacked a Chinese force on the same island with overwhelming firepower. After the fighting was over, according to one Soviet source (speaking, of course, off the record), there was nothing left of the Chinese but their belt buckles. This response, the effect of which was reinforced by subsequent Soviet behavior to be described shortly, threw Peking into a state of alarm. It probably set in motion the political decline of Lin Piao, who had carelessly exposed his country to serious risks for no adequate reason. Soon after the two clashes, former Foreign Minister Chen Yi, a man with extensive military as well as diplomatic experience, was made a Vice Chairman of the Party's powerful Military Affairs Commission, which was chaired by Lin Piao, presumably in order to balance and restrain Lin's radical fundamentalism. The Ninth Party Congress was postponed once more.

It is not clear whether there was any real basis for Peking's fear of a Soviet attack at this time. If there was, it is obvious that the doves in the Kremlin managed to prevail over the hawks; and it is not difficult to see why. Whatever the justification for it in Moscow's eyes, a major Soviet attack on China would create serious difficulties for the attackers as well as the defenders, Soviet strategic superiority notwith-standing. Indeed, the dissenting Soviet historian Amalrik has gone so far as to predict the break-up of the Soviet Union in the event of a Sino-Soviet war. Soviet territory would probably be exposed to a degree of Chinese nuclear and conventional retaliation. China's defensive capabilities against a Soviet conventional attack, especially an at-tempted penetration in depth, are formidable. The costs and strains of such a war on the Soviet political system and economy, even if they held together, would be enormous. Moscow's relations with the United States, Japan, other Communist Parties, and the rest of the world as well would be complicated and damaged to an unpredictable, but almost certainly substantial, degree.

Above all, there was the danger of driving Peking into the arms of the United States, a danger to which Moscow had been sensitive ever since about 1966. The Kremlin doves probably seized on a speech by Senator Edward M. Kennedy on March 20, in which he cited the Ussuri clashes as a reason for cultivating Peking, in order to reinforce their own arguments for cooling the tension with China. If not, then it is at least an odd coincidence that on March 21, Premier Kosygin tried to telephone Peking in order to discuss means of working toward a resolution of the border crisis. He was told by the Chinese side, which probably drew the correct inference that his call indicated that a Soviet attack was not imminent, to communicate his ideas through diplomatic channels. On March 29, accordingly, the Soviet government issued a public statement proposing "consultations" on the border crisis and territorial dispute.

Since this demand was controversial in Peking, it was evaded for the time being. The Ninth Party Congress convened at last on April 1. The major report was delivered by Lin Piao in his capacity as Mao's chosen successor. He, or his colleagues perhaps, thought it advisable to insert in his long and angry denunciation of the Soviet Union a statement indicating a willingness on Peking's part to take the old Sino-Russian boundary treaties, "unequal" though they were, "as the basis" for a new treaty. In other words, Peking was making clear the fact that it was not really demanding the return of large tracts of Soviet-controlled territory, apart from some fairly small areas along the Manchurian (islands in the Amur and Ussuri Rivers) and Central Asian sectors of the border, where Lin asserted that the Soviet Union was in occupation of land that had not been ceded in the "unequal" treaties and would have to be given back. The latter allegation was presumably a sop to Chinese national pride and to radical anti-Soviet sentiment, and a means of avoiding the appearance of passivity and appeasement on the border issue. It is interesting that Moscow did not officially and publicly acknowledge until 1976—although it unquestionably under-stood—that Peking was not, in fact, claiming large tracts of Soviet territory, presumably because such an admission would have tended to remove the conveniently emotional issue from the Soviet propaganda arsenal.

Whatever Moscow's actual view of Chinese intentions, it was de-termined to force Peking into "consultations" on the border issue as soon as practicable, probably in the hope of preempting and defusing to the extent possible the development of a close Sino-American relationship. Furthermore, Moscow wanted to initiate SALT negotia-tions with the United States now that it had attained approximate strategic parity, but was reluctant to do so before beginning talks with Peking, because of the danger of exposing itself to charges that Russia found it easier to deal with the American "imperialists" than with the "Socialist" Chinese. With typical Soviet heavyhandedness, very great pressures were employed to force Peking into talks. They produced the desired results, but at the same time pushed Peking closer to the United States.

Moscow began to reinforce its conventional and nuclear forces in the Mongolian People's Republic and on Soviet territory near the Chinese border, without making significant subtractions from its units facing NATO. By about 1973, Soviet forces near the Chinese border stood at nearly 50 divisions, supported by a formidable array of air power, strategic and tactical nuclear weapons, and the like. At about that time, the Chinese border region became a preferred maneuver area for Soviet—and reportedly also some East European—units. On June 13, 1969, Moscow issued a statement demanding, in superficially polite language but with menacing undertones, that Peking agree to "consultations" within two or three months. In the absence of any reply to this statement, Soviet units on August 13 (the two-month deadline) occupied a hill two kilometers on the Chinese side of the border in western Sinkiang, and defied the Chinese to dislodge them. Toward the end of August, midway between the two- and three-month deadlines, *Pravda* published an alarming editorial on the possibility of a Sino-Soviet war, while Moscow secretly queried some European Communist Parties and the United States government as to their reaction in the same eventuality. The American response is not publicly known for certain. According to one account, the White House ignored the Soviet inquiry; according to others, there was a strongly negative response. An American strategic alert at about that time may have been intended as a warning to Moscow in connection with the Sino-Soviet border crisis.

For military reasons, Peking was in no position to risk war. But for political reasons, it was not yet able to accede to the demands for "consultations." Peking's dilemma was eased by a fortuitous event, the death of Ho Chi Minh on September 3. Of all other Communist countries, North Vietnam was probably the one most anxious that there not be a Sino-Soviet war. If there were a war, North Vietnam would have to declare for one side or the other, something that it had managed to avoid doing during the course of the Sino-Soviet dispute to date; and Soviet and probably also Chinese equipment would no longer move across China by rail. During the funeral observances for Ho, the North Vietnamese pressed Kosygin, who headed the Soviet delegation, and his Chinese counterparts to avoid war. The Chinese side agreed that Kosygin could visit Peking on his way home for talks with Chou En-lai. This he did on September 11, only two days before the three-month deadline. According to a later Chinese statement (November 6, 1974), Kosygin agreed to a ceasefire and a mutual withdrawal of troops from the border, as well as to a nonaggression pact. But the accuracy of this account is doubtful. More probably, Chou demanded a ceasefire and a troop withdrawal and Kosygin repeated the demand for "consultations." In any event, there was no agreement, if only because each man had to report back to his colleagues. Since the Soviet position had been made reasonably clear and was backed by an implicit threat of force, it was up to the Chinese side to develop an equally coherent position unless it preferred to risk war.

The first indication was that anti-Soviet sentiment was still in the ascendant in Peking. On September 16, the slogans for the forthcoming Chinese National Day (October 1) were published, and one of them suggested in militant Maoist language that Peking was defying Moscow to do its worst. The next day, the London *Evening News* carried an article by its "Moscow correspondent," the celebrated KGB agent Victor Louis, to the effect that the Soviet leadership was still seriously contemplating an invasion of China or a "surgical strike" against its nuclear installations, or both. This article may have provided the moderates or doves in Peking, probably led by Chou En-lai, with the additional argument they needed. On September 18, a message went to Moscow; its contents are unknown, but were probably somewhat conciliatory—although evidently not conciliatory enough, since Moscow is not known to have made any reply. On October 6, another message was sent by the Chinese side. This one was evidently acceptable; at any rate, both sides announced on October 7 that they had just agreed to hold negotiations (not mere "consultations") on the border issue at the Deputy Foreign Minister level in the near future, and in Peking (the Soviets had been demanding Moscow). At the same time, however, Peking characteristically issued a statement insisting on its own version of the territorial dispute (in particular, on the "unequal" nature of the old boundary treaties), and on the proposition that "irreconcilable differences of principle" (including, but not necessarily restricted to, ideology) still separated the two sides.

The Border Negotiations

The talks got under way on October 20, and have proceeded at intervals ever since. Basically, they have been deadlocked from the start. Peking demanded—at any rate down to 1974, when the demand seems to have been dropped—a new boundary treaty that would brand the old treaties as "unequal," an admission that would be offensive to Soviet national pride. The Chinese side has also been insisting on a ceasefire, and a mutual troop withdrawal of 50 kilometers on each side of the border in areas where the location of the border is agreed; and where it is not, the whole of the disputed area would be evacuated by the forces of both sides. This demand for troop withdrawals is unacceptable to Moscow, at least pending a final settlement, both because its acceptance would take much of the pressure off the Chinese, and because a 50-kilometer withdrawal would leave Soviet units almost standing on the Trans-Siberian Railway in some areas. The Soviet side has been demanding essentially a reaffirmation of the status quo, and has refused to concede that the old treaties are "unequal."

By 1971, however, the Soviet side had begun to agree that the Manchurian sector of the border could be drawn, in accordance with international custom, along the main channel of the Amur and Ussuri Rivers, rather than along the Manchurian bank as Moscow had been insisting up to then; this concession gave Damansky/Chen Pao Island to the Chinese. There was to be one exception, however—Bear Island, the large island at the confluence of the Amur and Ussuri, which is very close to the important Soviet city of Khabarovsk. Moscow has insisted on retaining possession of this island, even though it lies on the Manchurian side of the main channel.

In mid-January 1971, probably in order to discourage a Chinese alignment with the United States, Brezhnev secretly proposed a non-aggression pact to Peking. The offer was rejected as meaningless, both then and when it was repeated publicly in 1973. Meanwhile, however, a modest trend toward the normalization of intergovernmental relations, apart from the border question, had set in. In October-November 1970, ambassadors were exchanged for the first time since 1966, and a trade agreement signed. Sino-Soviet trade had fallen to a level slightly lower than Soviet-Albanian trade ($30-40 million per year); but it began to rise after 1970 to a level of a few hundred million dollars a year both ways, approximating Peking's trade with one of the major West European countries.

The Fall of Lin Piao

As already indicated, the confrontation with the Soviet Union was a major issue in Peking's elite politics. The radicals were (and probably still are) basically opposed to the border talks with the Soviet "revisionists." The moderates, on the other hand, regard them as an essential form of insurance against war. There probably was (and is) little if any outright pro-Soviet feeling in Peking; but there have been disagreements over whether to manage the Soviet problem primarily on an ideological or pragmatic basis, and if the latter, then over how far detente should be carried. After Lin Piao's death on September 12, 1971, his opponents, led by Mao Tse-tung and Chou En-lai, charged that he had been pro-Soviet and had died in an airplane crash in the Mongolian People's Republic while trying to defect to the Soviet Union. The charge that Lin was pro-Soviet is contradicted by a good deal of evidence, including the negative Soviet attitude toward him. It has also been denied by Yang Yung in the interview already referred to, and is so inherently implausible that the crash had to be staged somehow, and the charge of attempted defection raised, in order to make it more nearly credible and to blacken Lin's memory. No other high ranking Chinese leader is known to have tried to defect to the Soviet Union in recent years, even border region "powerholders" who faced overthrow during the Cultural Revolution. The accusation of pro-Soviet sympathies against Lin is rendered even more implausible by its association with other fantastic charges, for example that he had been an incompetent military commander and had tried to assassinate Mao three times before attempting to flee the country.

It is not necessary to reconstruct here a reasonable interpretation of Lin Piao's fall and death; it will suffice to discuss those aspects that bear on Sino-Soviet relations. Lin almost certainly opposed the idea of an opening to the United States, even for the purpose of coping with the "social-imperialists." One of the main evidences of this is a speech by Lin's colleague and fellow-purgee, Chief of Staff Huang Yung-sheng, on July 31, 1971, after the first Kissinger visit to Peking, in which Huang excoriated both the United States and the Soviet Union as imminent threats to China. Lin probably reacted to the Soviet offer of a nonaggression pact in 1971, not by favoring acceptance, but by arguing that the offer indicated that the Soviets were still irresolute paper bears, despite their military power and seemingly threatening behavior. Hence, there was no need for the ideologically distasteful opening to the United States, which was regarded by Chou En-lai as necessary and presumably accepted by Mao. Lin, in short, clung inflexibly to a dual adversary strategy, and apparently believed that ideological correctness and political sophistication would enable Peking to maintain a simultaneous struggle against both the superpowers. His primitiveness in this regard undoubtedly contributed heavily to his fall, although it was not necessarily the main reason for it.

After his death, Peking proceeded rapidly with its opening to the United States, and settled down to the maintenance of what appeared to be a confrontation with the Soviet Union of possibly indefinite duration. Moscow necessarily had to do the same, although the option of war of course remained open to it, at least in theory. For the time being, Soviet pressures along the Sino-Soviet border were effectively containing China by deterring Chinese military moves against any part of Asia, Soviet or non-Soviet; although it was by no means clear that Peking would actually attempt conventional military action against any part of Asia in the absence of such containment, especially in view of the continuing American commitment to the security of non-Communist Asia.

4

Maneuvering For Position

Once something like a standoff along the border had been achieved by about the end of 1969, China and the Soviet Union began to engage in more and more complicated maneuvers against each other, with the obvious aim of getting significant political advantages without war. The most important single arena was what might be called competitive detente with the United States.

Peking's Opening to the United States

As the weaker party to the Sino-Soviet confrontation, Peking was probably more eager than Moscow in cultivating detente with the United States. Competition with Moscow was not the only motive; other considerations included progress toward the "liberation" of Taiwan through erosion of the American commitment to the Republic of China, and technological contact with the United States. American politics and foreign policy—in particular, the Nixon Administration's desire for Chinese help in ending the Vietnam War, and for leverage in dealing with the Soviet Union—created some American vulnerabilities and exposed the United States to Chinese manipulation. On the other hand, Chinese politics created problems for Sino-American detente inasmuch as the powerful faction of Maoist radicals (apart from Mao himself, it appears) were basically opposed to it. This factor helps to explain why the detente was on obviously shaky ground until Lin Piao's fall in September 1971. Thereafter, detente progressed much more smoothly for about two years, and then again showed signs of strain after the radicals began to reassert themselves in the Summer of 1973.

The presence of others does not affect the priority of the Soviet factor in Chinese calculations. Peking did not want or expect a miltary alliance or guarantee from the United States against the Soviet Union; the domestic politics and foreign policies of both China and the United States forbade such a commitment. But Peking evidently hoped for what might be called a counterweight to Soviet pressures on China in the form of a Sino-American relationship sufficiently improved so as to create in the minds of the Soviet leadership a significant uncertainty about the probable American reaction to a Soviet attack on China. This seems to have been achieved until at least 1973. There was the further consideration that Peking did not want to permit the Soviet Union to achieve a closer relationship with the United States than China had itself.

The first thing was to get President Nixon to come to China—a fairly easy task since he was eager to come. The Chinese invitation was first made public in mid-July 1971, at the end of Kissinger's first, secret, visit to China. It was confirmed during the second Kissinger visit in October, and the President came in late February 1972. It is not necessary to go into the Peking summit as a whole. Its Soviet aspect, which is what concerns us here, was actually rather subtle and indirect. For each side, the main hoped-for effect on Moscow was simply the fact of the summit; neither wanted to concede leverage to the other or to provoke Moscow by explicity stressing the anti-Soviet purpose of the summit. The main way in which this purpose showed itself was in a single passage in the final document, the socalled Shanghai Communique; this was the "antihegemony" clause, in which both sides agreed that "neither should seek hegemony in the Asia-Pacific region, and each is opposed to efforts by any other country or group of countries to establish such hegemony." This clause not only covered the Soviet Union, but was directed specifically against it, at least in the Chinese understanding.

The other major early landmark in the Sino-American detente was the agreement of February 1973 to exchange liaison offices, which were embassies in everything but name, but which could not be called embassies because US diplomatic and security ties with the Republic of China prevented the establishment of formal diplomatic relations.

After about the middle of 1973, the Sino-American detente made no further advances, and in fact showed some signs of strain and ineffectiveness. One of the reasons, as already suggested, was the radical resurgence in China. Another was Peking's objections to US cultivation of detente with the Soviet Union and to the priority that the United States appeared to give to it as against detente with China. A third was the need of first the Nixon and then the Ford Administrations to maintain conservative political support in view of Watergate and the approach of the 1976 election, and the fact that conservative opinion in the United States tends to support the Republic of China. A fourth was Moscow's recovery, after about 1973, from the initial shock of the Sino-American detente, its realization of the limitations involved, and the resulting decline in the effectiveness of Sino-American detente as a constraint on Soviet behavior.

Of all these problems, Peking was probably most troubled by the belief that the United States was no longer holding up its end of the contest with the Soviet Union in the strategic arms race, in Europe or in the Third World, and was of declining value as a counterweight to the Soviet Union. This view was expressed at the highest level to a number of visiting Americans, official and unofficial, and in particular to Secretary Kissinger in October 1975, to President Ford in December 1975, and to former President Nixon in February 1976. By contrast, Peking clearly approved of the tough anti-Soviet posture taken by such men as former Secretary of Defense James R. Schlesinger and Senator Henry M. Jackson.

Soviet Detente Strategy

There is no need here for an analysis of all aspects of Moscow's motives in seeking detente with the United States; not all of them relate directly to China. In a general sense, however, the totality of Soviet motives is relevant to China. The Kremlin wants to ensure, in so far as possible, that it has at least as close a relationship with the United States as China—provided, of course, that the effort to develop such a relationship does not impose unacceptable damage to vital Soviet interests.

The main general purposes of Soviet detente strategy appear to be to avoid a major war with the United States, to achieve and maintain strategic parity with the United States but not at levels that would exhaust the Soviet economy (hence the need for SALT), and to establish beneficial economic and technological contacts with the United

States. The last motive became especially important after the Polish riots of December 1970. Moscow has been trying, through its economic opening to the industralized countries, to avoid both a thoroughgoing reform movement of the kind that swept Czechoslovakia in 1968, and a protest from below over inadequate living standards such as occurred in Poland. It is probably not a coincidence that Brezhnev's first major public indication (apart from the initiation of the SALT talks in November 1969) of an interest in detente with the United States was given at the 24th Party Congress (March 1971), only a few months after the Polish riots.

Although none of these considerations is directly related to China, it is clear that Soviet detente strategy as a whole has been closely linked to Sino-Soviet and Sino-American relations. The announcement of the first Kissinger visit to Peking (July 1971) struck Moscow like a thunderbolt, and galvanized it into a frenzy of progaganda and diplomatic activity over the next few months, much of it with an obviously anti-Chinese purpose. An excellent example is the Soviet-Indian treaty of friendship, signed on August 9, 1971, after two years of footdragging on both sides, which helped greatly to guarantee Peking's noninvolvement in the Indo-Pakistani War that broke out the following December. The Soviet invitation to President Nixon to visit Moscow for a summit conference was issued in October 1971, by which time it had become clear that the Chinese invitation to a similar summit in Peking had not been cancelled on account of the Lin Piao affair. There is little doubt that Moscow's decision not to cancel or disrupt its May 1972 summit with Nixon on account of his renewed bombing of North Vietnam and the mining of Haiphong was largely due to a determination not to be left as odd man out in the wake of the Peking summit.

For another year, until after the establishment of liaison offices in Peking and Washington, Moscow continued to be impressed by the significance of the Sino-American detente, and to be influenced by it—at least to some degree—in its policy toward both the parties. On May 13, 1973, for example, two days before the arrival of David Bruce in Peking to head the United States Liaison Office there, two Soviet naval vessels circumnavigated Taiwan—the first time that Soviet ships had done this. The intended message seemed to be that if the United States could establish ties with "its" Chinese in Peking, so might the Soviet Union with "its" Chinese in Taipei. Indeed, there has been some evidence, and much speculation, since about 1968 that something might be developing between Moscow and Taipei as an outgrowth of the confrontation between Moscow and Peking.

Soon afterward, however, the Soviet Union seems to have relaxed about the Sino-American detente. The main apparent reasons have already been given: the simple passage of time, the radical resurgence in China, and the signs of strain and stasis in the Sino-American relationship. This changing Soviet perception probably contributed to making Moscow less careful in its cultivation of detente with the United States; some well-known examples of this new tendency were its abrogation of the 1972 Soviet-American commercial treaty in January 1975, and the Soviet-Cuban intervention in Angola. Nothing about the Ford summit in Peking or the second Nixon visit to China is likely to have convinced Moscow that the Sino-American relationship was growing stronger. On the contrary, statements made by Chinese leaders on those occasions doubtless encouraged the Kremlin by underlining how worried Peking was about the Soviet-American detente, and about the inadequate performance of the United States in balancing and coping with the Soviet Union. On the other hand, recent strains in Soviet-American relations must, in turn, have given some encouragement to Peking.

"Collective Security" in Europe and Asia

In the post-World War II period, the Soviet Union first raised the idea of some sort of collective security arrangement for Europe in 1954, as a counter to West Germany's admission to NATO. The proposal took on more vigor in 1967 as a Soviet and East European counter to West German *Ostpolitik*. There is no need to go into all the subsequent history of the proposal, or to analyze the resulting Helsinki Agreement of 1975. The idea gathered momentum after the invasion of Czechoslovakia, and its two major early fruits were the Soviet-West German treaty of August 1970 and the four-power agreement on West Berlin of September 1971.

Although the point would probably be impossible to prove, there is now fairly general acceptance among Western observers that Moscow's main purpose in seeking detente, "collective security," and the like in Europe has been to reduce the likelihood of tension or war in the region while Moscow concentrated on its Chinese problem by pinning Peking militarily to the border and competing vigorously with it elsewhere, notably in Asia. An indication of the Chinese aspects of Moscow's

European policy is the following revealing provision in the Helsinki Agreement regarding maneuvers, which must have been inserted at the initiative of the Soviet Union:

> In the case of a participating State whose territory extends beyond Europe, prior notification need be given only of maneuvers which take place in an area within 250 kilometers from its frontier facing or shared with any other European participating State . . . the participating State need not, however, give notification in cases in which that area is also contiguous to the participating State's frontier facing or shared with a non-European nonparticipating State.

The most obvious applicability of the exclusion is, of course, to Soviet maneuvers near the Chinese border.

Since the beginnning of the Sino-Soviet confrontation, Peking has been eager to see Western Europe united, NATO strong, and the United States militarily present in Europe. This is roughly the opposite of the Soviet position. Just as Moscow wants to be able to divert as much attention from Europe as possible, Peking wants the Soviet Union to be distracted by Europe to the greatest possible extent.

Since the invasion of Czechoslovakia, Peking has been able to exert little influence in Eastern Europe, except to some extent in Yugoslavia and Albania. The reality of Soviet power is too overwhelming. Even Albania has shown some signs of interest in improving its relations with the Soviet Union. Peking is clearly worried about the possibility of Soviet pressures on Yugoslavia after the death of Tito, and about the potential growth of Soviet influence in southern Europe resulting from the improved political position of basically pro-Soviet Communist Parties, notably in Italy.

When Moscow succeeded in convening an international conference of Communist Parties (except for the pro-Chinese CPs) in June 1969, after a seven-month delay caused by the invastion of Czechoslovakia, one of its main purposes was apparently to get a resolution condemning Peking for its behavior along the Sino-Soviet border. This it failed to do, evidently because a number of Communist Parties—notably the Rumanian—objected to this transparent Soviet effort to manipulate the Chinese bogey so as to rally other CPs, especially those of the Warsaw Pact, under Soviet leadership. As a second best, Brezhnev fell back on his celebrated but vague statement, "We are of the opinion that the course of events raises the question of a system of collective security in Asia."

Although this proposal has been made slightly more explicit in subsequent Soviet pronouncements, and although it has been vigorously propagated in Asia, its content remains vague. Given Moscow's obsession with the Sino-Soviet confrontation, espousal of the idea would be enough to raise the suspicion that it is anti-Chinese in some sense, or at least that it is somehow designed to restrain, in an era of American disengagement from Asia, the "expansionist" tendencies which Moscow attributes to Peking. Certainly the Chinese have denounced the Soviet "collective security" proposal as if it were directed against them, even though Moscow insists that it is not and claims to want Peking as a participant. To date, Chinese opposition has been enough to prevent any other East Asian government from showing interest in the proposal. None of them wants to purchase a virtually unknown quantity at the price of Chinese hostility.

Although the Soviet Union conducts much of its Asian policy under the strange banner of collective security, with the Helsinki Agreement cited as a model for Asia, in reality Soviet rivalry with China in the region aims at more specific targets. Peking wants to include an "antihegemony" clause in the peace treaty it is negotiating with Japan, and is trying to provide Japan with a significant fraction of its oil imports. Moscow objects strongly to the "antihegemony" clause, although its objections are not likely to be effective in the long run. It is also blocking its own peace treaty with Japan by its refusal to return the socalled Northern Territories (four small islands lying between Hokkaido and the Kuriles) to Japan, while at the same time withholding satisfactory and dependable commitments from Japan regarding deliveries of oil and other industrial raw materials. Peking's standing and influence in Japan are considerably greater than Moscow's. The main Soviet asset is Japan's awareness of Moscow's power and its interest in Siberian resources.

In North Korea, Peking has been somewhat more adept at cultivating the incredibly difficult Kim Il-sung. Neither of the two Communist giants has any desire, however, to see him attack South Korea again. Both want stability to continue on the Peninsula; and both therefore appear to want the United States to retain its military presence in South Korea, despite propaganda demands for American withdrawal.

In Indochina, Hanoi's fear of Peking, as well as Moscow's superior ability to provide aid in the form of heavy military and industrial equipment, have given the Soviet Union greater influence than China in the Democratic Republic of Vietnam. The same holds true of Laos, mainly because of the strong Vietnamese influence on the new Communist regime in that country. In Cambodia, on the other hand, the new regime is profoundly suspicious of the Democratic Republic of Vietnam, and thus anti-Soviet and pro-Chinese. An informal combination of China, Cambodia, and Thailand seems to be emerging as a counterweight to the equally informal grouping of Vietnam, Laos, and the Soviet Union.

On January 20, 1974, Peking drove a South Vietnamese force off the Paracel Islands in the South China Sea, which China claims and has occupied ever since. One likely reason for this action was that Hanoi, too, claims the islands and is regarded by Peking as dangerously pro-Soviet. The Chinese may be concerned over the possibility that Hanoi might grant Moscow naval facilities at Camranh Bay in the name of "collective security."

Elsewhere in Southeast Asia, Chinese influence for a variety of reasons is generally greater than Soviet. Peking's diplomacy is more skillful, its ethnic and cultural affinities are much greater, and it has had the good sense to keep its manipulation of local Chinese communities and its support for Communist insurgencies within reasonable bounds, at least in recent years. Three of the ASEAN (Association of Southeast Asian Nations) states—Malaysia, the Philippines, and Thailand—recognized Peking in 1974-75. Nearly all the Southeast Asian countries would like to improve their relations with China; and Peking generally reciprocates this feeling, if only because of its desire to stay ahead of the Soviet Union in the region. The main holdout is Indonesia, which like the Democratic Republic of Vietnam tends to see China as a rival for leadership in the region, as well as something of a threat; for external support (arms and so forth), Indonesia relies on the United States rather than on the Soviet Union.

This is obviously not true of India, which has "tilted" toward the Soviet Union for many years. To cope with the Indo-Soviet combination and to promote its own interests in the Subcontinent, Peking established a close relationship with Pakistan in the early 1960s. Since Pakistan's humiliating defeat by India in 1971, China has established diplomatic and otherwise friendly relations with Iran; and in various ways, Peking and Teheran are attempting to support Pakistan and shield it against possible Indian or Afghan pressures. On the other hand, India does not want to be dependent on the Soviet Union, and Peking in turn would like to encourage India not to be. Such consideration as these appear to account for the decision by India and China in the Spring of 1976 to exchange ambassadors for the first time since 1963. The overthrow of the pro-Indian government of Sheik Mujib in Bangladesh in August 1975 was a setback for India and the Soviet Union, and at least something of a gain for China and the United States.

Rivalry in the Third World

Sino-Soviet competition in the Third World dates from the late 1950s, and has become increasingly important during the current stage of confrontation between Peking and Moscow. The Chinese portray themselves as a friend and champion—but not explicitly as the leader— of the "small and medium states," including those of the Third World, and as a "developing Socialist country belonging to the Third World."

The Soviet Union maintains a growing presence in the Indian Ocean through the movements of its fleet and its influence in certain of the littoral countries, such as India and Somalia. This presence is clearly competitive with both the United States and China. For its part, Peking does not as yet have a navy capable of showing the flag in the Indian Ocean, and it must rely for influence in this important region largely on cultivating selected littoral states, notably Sri Lanka and Tanzania. Sino-Soviet rivalry in the Middle East has not been especially intense, since Peking has no influence, and no opportunity for acquiring influence, that is at all comparable with the Soviet Union or the United States. The most important recent development in the region relevant to the Sino-Soviet dispute is almost certainly President Sadat's turn away from the Soviet Union, which China of course has welcomed. It is interesting that China and Yugoslavia, both of them countries threatened by the Soviet Union, have agreed to supply spare parts for some of Egypt's Soviet-built jet aircraft; India has refused to do so, apparently at Soviet insistence.

The most important arena of Sino-Soviet interaction in the Third World, apart from Asia, is probably Africa. In Angola, limited Chinese support via Zaire for Holden Roberto's National Front, which Peking tried unsuccessfully to persuade to wage a "people's war," was no match for Neto's Popular Movement and the Cuban "Afrika Corps," with its heavy Soviet weapons. With or without the Cubans, a similar pattern may also emerge in Mozambique, where shipments of Soviet equipment seem to be increasing Moscow's influence on the anti-Rhodesian guerrillas.

Bilateral Interaction: Military Considerations

For a time in 1973, beginning in the Spring, Peking began to indicate indirectly that it possessed what it considered a second-strike deterrent against the Soviet Union and, partly for that reason, to state that the main thrust of Soviet "expansionism" was no longer toward China but elsewhere, mainly toward Europe. In addition to the military factor, there were probably political motives for this statement, which came from Chou En-lai. Conceivably it may have been an olive branch, at least in a modified form consistent with Chou's established strategy of mollifying Moscow from time to time. This seems improbable, however, inasmuch as Moscow reacted negatively to the proposition that the main thrust of its "expansionism" was toward Europe. Another possibility is that Peking wanted to discourage the United States and Western Europe from relaxing their anti-Soviet vigilance on the theory that China was now absorbing Moscow's excess energies. Another plausible explanation is that since the fall of Lin Piao, Chou had been making substantial cuts in China's military budget, presumably on the assumption that they could be compensated for with such other assets as the Sino-American detente; and he may have believed that the cuts could not be defended at home if the Soviet Union were still portrayed as an active threat to China. Finally, Chou had previously been using the Soviet threat, real or alleged, as a basis for demanding greater subordination to Peking from the military region commanders, who had virtually dominated the provinces since 1967. This problem appears to have been brought under control in 1973, when eight of the most powerful military region commanders were suddenly transferred in December.

On March 14, 1974, while Peking was still in this relatively confident mood, three Soviet officers and their helicopter were captured on the Chinese side of the border between Sinkiang and Soviet Central Asia. Moscow made no effort to rescue them before capture, despite their appeals for help, but then immediately demanded their release on the ground that they had been on a medical mission and had overflown the border by accident. Peking refused to release them and insisted, with some plausibility, that they had been engaged in espionage. It was in this tense atmosphere that a sizable armed clash (which neither side reported in the press) took place in April on the Sino-Mongolian border, the most sensitive sector of the entire frontier because of its proximity to Peking. The initiative in this engagement is unclear, but was probably Soviet. On May 3, Moscow warned of unspecified "inevitable consequences" if the helicopter crew was not released. But the Chinese stood firm, largely no doubt for internal political reasons centering on radical objections to anything smacking of appeasement of "social-imperialism."

Under these circumstances, the atmosphere along the border remained tense. There were reports in 1974 and 1975 of some East European units (probably Polish and East German) taking part in maneuvers near the border. Peking claimed, and Moscow denied, that there was a clash on the Sinkiang frontier in February 1976. Meanwhile, each side continued to propagandize the minorities (Kazakhs, Kirghiz, and others) on the other side. Peking staged an elaborate celebration of the 20th anniversary of the Sinkiang Uighur Autonomous Region on October 1, 1975, in the course of which even more than the usual propaganda was made about the Soviet threat to the region. This may have been designed in part as a distraction from the mounting tension in Peking between the moderates and the radicals.

The confident Chinese mood of 1975 appeared to deteriorate under the impact of these strains, and of other developments that Peking regarded as even more serious. One was the Soviet-American summit conference of November 1974; and what perturbed Peking was not so much the choice of Vladivostok as the conference site as the fact that this was the fourth Soviet-American summit since the Peking summit of February 1972. Peking promptly invited President Ford to Peking; but it could not erase the suspicion that the United States considered detente with the Soviet Union as more important than detente with China, and that the United States was not doing enough to hold up its end of the struggle with Moscow. Another sign of the same thing in Peking's eyes was the collapse of the American-supported Indochinese states in 1975. Not only did this development speak poorly for the resoluteness and effectiveness of American Far Eastern policy. It also removed one Soviet inhibition against an attack on China, namely, the desirability from Moscow's point of view of not impeding Hanoi's war effort or damaging its own standing in the eyes of the international left by attacking China while the war in Vietnam was unfinished.

Meanwhile, some developments of possible long-range strategic importance were under way. The Soviet Union was beginning to build a new railway line across Eastern Siberia to the Pacific, the socalled Baikal-Amur Railway, which would be farther north and therefore more secure than the relatively vulnerable Trans-Siberian line. Moscow tried to get some Japanese financing for this project, but was refused; Tokyo evidently had in mind not only its own interests, but Chinese views as well. Whether or not China has a nuclear second-strike capability and therefore a minimum deterrent, it appears to have at least the beginnings of an overhead reconnaissance capability; its fifth earth satellite was orbited in December 1975. Peking was apparently thinking less in terms of defense in depth and "people's war" in the event of a Soviet attack, and more in terms of border defense. It certainly did not want to lose Manchuria, or Peking itself.

Bilateral Interaction: Political Considerations

Since at least as long ago as 1969, Moscow and Peking have continued to perceive each other as potentially irrational, and therefore as requiring to be constrained by any and all available means. This perception appears genuine, even though it is overstated by both sides for propaganda effect. Each side charges the other with being a major, if not the major, force for war in the contemporary world. Moscow insists that China is trying to incite war between the United States and the Soviet Union. What Peking has said on this subject, since 1970, is that there will be such a war "some day" unless it is prevented by "revolution" (in the two superpowers, evidently), and that revolution is the "main trend" in the world today. But this is obviously Maoist rhetoric that does not deserve to be taken seriously—and probably is not taken seriously—by any one, even Moscow, with the possible exception of some of the radicals in China.

In March 1972, Brezhnev reversed a previous position and accepted a Chinese demand of ten years' standing by conceding that Sino-Soviet relations could be governed by "peaceful coexistence" rather than by "proletarian" (or "Socialist") "internationalism," as would be normal between "Socialist" states. This, for whatever it was worth, was probably designed to balance American acceptance in the Shanghai Communique of Peking's similar and favorite formula for relations between states having "different social systems," the "five principles of peaceful coexistence."

In 1973, Moscow began to make public offers of a nonaggression pact, only to be rebuffed by Peking. The Soviet side was making an obvious effort to appear the more reasonable of the adversaries. Beginning in 1972, Soviet propaganda began to portray the Treaty of Nerchinsk (1689), which had cost Russia control of the territory north of the Amur River until the mid-19th century, as "unequal" because allegedly imposed by superior Manchu forces. Peking rebutted the argument, but was evidently impressed by it.

In early November 1974, Kosygin repeated the offer of a non-aggression pact, and was echoed by the Mongolian delegate to the United Nations. The Vladivostok summit was approaching, and it would be advantageous to both Moscow and Peking not to appear so immobilized by an unbridgeable Sino-Soviet dispute that the United States could manipulate either or both parties to it. In this spirit, Peking sent a relatively friendly message to Moscow on November 6, the eve of the anniversary of the October Revolution. Without referring to the Soviet proposal for a nonaggression pact, or to the "unequal" treaties, the Chinese message proposed a nonaggression pact as part of a larger package that also included an agreement on a ceasefire and a mutual troop withdrawal along the border, and a boundary settlement. It claimed, with what degree of accuracy is not known, that Kosygin had accepted the entire package in September 1969. This message was given little publicity in Peking, probably because it was controversial there. Similarly, the Soviet side did not reprint the most important part of the message. Nevertheless, Brezhnev waited until November 26, 1974, after the Vladivostok summit, to reject it. Presumably he wanted to enjoy in the meantime the advantage of having the American side less sure that the Sino-Soviet dispute was incurable. Brezhnev repeated on November 26 the exaggerated and oversimplified claim that the Chinese were demanding large tracts of Soviet territory. It was probably to this statement that Chou En-lai referred in his report of January 13, 1975, to the National People's Congress:

> They (the Soviets) even deny the existence of the disputed areas on the Sino-Soviet border, and they even refuse to do anything about such matters as the disengagement of the armed forces of the two sides in the disputed areas on the

border and the prevention of armed conflicts; instead, they talk profusely about empty treaties on the nonuse of force against each other and mutual nonaggression. So what can their real intention be if not to deceive the Soviet people and world public opinion? We wish to advise the Soviet leadership to sit down and negotiate honestly, do something to solve a bit of the problem, and stop playing such deceitful tricks.

The "honest" negotiations for which Chou claimed to be calling have not yet occurred.

On December 27, 1975, Peking released the Soviet helicopter crew taken in March 1974. Investigation had allegedly revealed that Soviet claims as to the helicopter's supposed medical mission were credible. No explanation was offered for the extraordinary length of time required to verify the crew's story. Regardless of this and the real facts of the case, the release must be seen as some kind of gesture. It took place about three weeks after the disappointing summit conference with President Ford, and it was probably designed, at least in part, to startle the United States into doing better against the Soviet Union by suggesting the possibility of a Sino-Soviet rapprochement. In reality, there is no convincing evidence that such a rapprochement is imminent, or that one is seriously contemplated on either side. Even though Brezhnev, in his report to the 25th Party Congress (February 24, 1976), repeated Moscow's willingness to base its relations with Peking on "peaceful coexistence," he reiterated that the Chinese were "seeking to provoke a world war in order to gain advantage thereby," and insisted that, as far as further steps toward a Sino-Soviet rapprochement were concerned, "The ball is in the Chinese court."

At the time Brezhnev spoke, however, some events of great potential importance for Sino-Soviet relations had just occurred. The death of Chou En-lai on January 8, 1976, was bound to be seen in Moscow, with at least partial accuracy, as opening a period of instability in Chinese politics during which some fresh initiatives of the carrot-and-stick variety might bring important gains for Soviet interests. This feeling must have been intensified when, later that month, Vice Premier Teng Hsiao-p'ing, who had appeared to be the man most likely to succeed Chou En-lai as Premier, began to lose ground in the resurgent political infighting in Peking. His dismissal from his various important posts was announced on April 7, two days after a riot in Tien An Men Square apparently organized by his supporters. Even though Teng was probably seen by the radicals as too "soft" (or "capitulationist") toward the Soviet Union, he was almost certainly judged in Moscow as essentially an adversary. For one thing, he had taken a leading role in presenting Peking's case against Moscow in a variety of forums during the early 1960s. His removal, therefore, no matter how viewed in Peking, may well have appeared in Moscow as a development that made an improvement of Sino-Soviet relations at least a little easier.

A somewhat analogous event occurred shortly afterward on the Soviet side, with the death of Defense Minister and Politburo member Marshal Grechko on April 26. Whatever his actual views on China may have been, there are plausible reasons for believing that Peking considered him a hawk in this connection. He had been close to Brezhnev, whom Peking regards as an archenemy. He had been in office during the invasion of Czechoslovakia and the Sino-Soviet border crisis of 1969, the two episodes that established firmly in the Chinese consciousness the image of the Soviet Union as a mortal threat. He was the leader of an important military mission to India, a country that Peking thinks of as conspiring with the Soviet Union to contain China, at the time of the first clash on the Ussuri River (March 2, 1969). His death and replacement by a civilian must have appeared to at least some people in Peking as a moderately encouraging development; at any rate, Moscow probably expected it to be so received in Peking.

It was therefore not surprising that an important and relatively conciliatory article on Sino-Soviet relations appeared in *Pravda* on April 28, under a pseudonym ("I. Aleksandrov"). In addition to the death of Marshal Grechko, Peking's diplomatic success in establishing itself as at least a partial successor to Moscow in providing military equipment to Egypt may also have been a factor in making Moscow anxious to appear interested in an improvement of relations with Peking. Although the Aleksandrov article repeated Moscow's usual denunciation of Maoism and its refusal to accept a troop pullback prior to a border settlement, it conceded—apparently for the first time in a published Soviet statement—that Peking was claiming only 33,000 square kilometers of territory currently held by the Soviet Union, rather than 1.5 million square kilometers that Soviet propaganda had previously alleged.

The following day, an explosion occurred outside the Soviet Embassy in Peking. The Chinese authorities soon announced that it had been the work of a "counterrevolutionary saboteur," presumably Chinese, who had been killed in the explosion. This was considerably less than a precise identification, inasmuch as the term "counterrevolutionary saboteur" has been applied in Chinese propaganda to Teng Hsiao-p'ing since his fall. It would be reasonable to attribute the blast to someone connected with the radical faction who may have wanted to ensure that the Aleksandrov article did not lead to an improvement in Sino-Soviet relations. The event does not, however, appear to have created a serious crisis within the Chinese leadership. At any rate, the principal radicals were among those who appeared for the May Day celebrations, although security precautions on that occasion were unprecedentedly strict.

Obviously, the Sino-Soviet relationship is strongly influenced by internal political forces at work in both countries. On the Soviet side, Alexander Shelepin, who has appeared to be less anti-Chinese than most of his colleagues, was dropped from the Politburo in the Spring of 1975, although probably not primarily for that reason. The present (post-25th Congress) Politburo appears to be predominantly more anti-Western than anti-Chinese. In other words, they seem likely to believe that China, in spite of its internal problems, is too tough a nut to crack, politically and militarily, even though the current strategy of military deterrence and political competition must be maintained. The main opportunities for the expansion of Soviet influence, whether through local Communist Parties or otherwise, probably appear to be in the West, and—primarily at the West's expense—in the Third World.

On the Chinese side, Moscow claims to believe that Chou En-lai favored a more comprehensive normalization of relations with the Soviet Union than his colleagues would permit, and has circulated what purports to be a kind of testament by Chou to that effect. The document appears to be a fake, and the attribution of this view to Chou is very doubtful except as a plausible version of his possible long-term hopes. Soviet analysts have been correct, on the other hand, in maintaining that Teng Hsiao-p'ing was not likely to make the grade as Chou's successor. Moscow claims to believe that there are some "healthy forces" (its term for pro-Soviet local Communists) in Peking, especially among the military leadership, and this view finds fairly wide acceptance among Western analysts. It does seem probable that there are some Chinese military leaders, such as the recently rehabilitated former Chief of Staff Lo Jui-ch'ing, and perhaps some civilian moderates, who would like to see a reduction in the level of tension along the border and in general political relations with the Soviet Union. No one relishes the prospect of a losing war against a superior adversary; and in the case of the military, there may be some interest in spare parts and, if possible, even new advanced equipment from the Soviet Union.

There is no evidence or plausible reason for believing that such individuals favor major concessions to Moscow, however, at any rate not without equivalent concessions from the Soviet side. The radicals apparently support a continuation of the confrontation with the Soviet Union, short of war, on ideological and political grounds. During the barrage of charges of "capitulation" hurled at Teng Hsiao-p'ing and his fellow moderates in the Fall of 1975, an implied tendency to "capitulate" to the Soviet Union was one of the accusations. The release of the Soviet helicopter crew at the end of the year may also have been cited by the radicals as a case of "capitulation," and may have contributed to Teng's fall after January 1976.

It appears that the Soviet Union is waiting to see what happens in China after the death of Mao-Tse-tung, while in the meantime making the most of its opportunities in other areas. After Mao's death, there is certainly some possibility of improvement in Sino-Soviet relations, along lines that are discussed in Chapter 7. But there is at least one basic problem. Moscow is temperamentally incapable of working on an equal footing with any other country, Communist or non-Communist; and Peking is too strong to be coerced into, and too proud to accept voluntarily, a relationship of inferiority such as it tolerated temporarily in the 1950s.

5

The Short-Term Future:
Leadership Succession in
Moscow and Peking

The next few years will almost certainly see the retirement or death of Brezhnev and Mao Tse-tung, and it is likely that their departure will be a dominant feature of the political scene in both countries. This chapter considers the possible nature of this process and its implications for Sino-Soviet relations.

The Succession to Brezhnev

Since the fall of Khrushchev in 1964, the Soviet leadership has followed a policy of "stability of cadres," which means a low rate of turnover at the upper (but not always at the middle and lower) levels of the Party apparatus. There is no sign that this policy is likely to change in the near future, even after Brezhnev's departure.

This is not to say that there have been no recent changes at the Politburo level. There have been some, and they appear to be relevant both to the succession question and possibly to Sino-Soviet relations. One change has been the removal of D. S. Polyansky both from the Ministry of Agriculture and from the Politburo at the time of the 25th Party Congress (February 24-March 5, 1976), ostensibly because of the poor state of Soviet agriculture. In reality, his problem seems to have been more personal. It is significant that F. D. Kulakov, the member of the Secretariat charged with general supervision of agricultural affairs, has not suffered; and this strengthens the common belief that he is Brezhnev's favored candidate for the succession to the General Secretaryship, perhaps after a transitional period under elder statesmen A. P. Kirilenko and M. A. Suslov.

Perhaps the fastest-rising figure in the Soviet leadership in the past few years has been G. V. Romanov, the head of the Leningrad Party apparatus, who was elected a regular Politburo member after the 25th Party Congress, and who may be scheduled for transfer to Moscow. As in the case of others just below the top, his views on major policy questions, including Sino-Soviet relations, are not known.

The personnel change with perhaps the greatest significance for Sino-Soviet relations, as suggested in the previous chapter, has been the death of Defense Minister Marshal A. A. Grechko on April 26, 1976. His successor, the civilian D. F. Ustinov, who was elected to the Politburo after the 25th Congress, is not likely to be so hawklike, and hence so anti-Chinese, as Grechko, or so influential as his predecessor.

The Outlook for Soviet Politics and Foreign Policy

There is no convincing reason to expect anything very different from a continuation of the "stability of cadres" policy, and of stability in other major fields as well. The present situation, whose approximate continuation we may assume, can be summarized as follows.

The Soviet Union is controlled by a cumbersome and repressive Party and police dictatorship. Under these conditions, it has been impossible for an organized opposition to emerge. Nevertheless, there is considerable potential for disaffection among the national minorities, and even among Russian workers in the event of prolonged food shortages that could not be alleviated through imports. The economy is limping along under the impact of a labor shortage, excessive controls, a heavy military budget (about 11 percent of Gross National Product), and recurrent agricultural failures. Since the mid-1960s, the armed forces have been built up to a level of approximate strategic parity with the United States, and the aim seems to be a further build-up to a level of parity with the United States and China combined.

This military build-up has been used, and presumably will continue to be used, to promote Soviet security (through deterrence) and influence, and not necessarily to conduct actual military operations. Detente with the United States has been understood in Moscow rather narrowly, until now at any rate, to mean mainly the avoidance of a major war and the maintenance of beneficial economic and technological contacts. Meanwhile, the Soviet Union continues to seek advantage and influence at the expense of others, the United States included, under such labels as "ideological struggle," especially in the Third World and Europe (notably southern Europe). This is done, however, within the limits imposed by considerations of cost and of risk to more important objectives, especially security.

As we have seen, Soviet policy toward China may be described as watchful waiting and careful management, or more precisely as deterrence and competition in third areas, and of preparedness for any of the three major possible outcomes: war, detente, or a continuation of confrontation.

The Succession to Mao

No one could accuse the Chinese Communist Party of having observed the principle of "stability of cadres." Of the 17 men elected to the Politburo after the Eighth Party Congress (1956), only two (Liu Po-ch'eng and Li Hsien-nien) remain beside Mao Tse-tung; the others have been dropped, from natural or unnatural causes. Although the radicals remain strong in the Party leadership and presumably will continue so at least as long as Mao lives, and although the moderates suffered serious losses through the death of Chou En-lai and the purge of Teng Hsiao-p'ing in January 1976, on the whole the moderates are the stronger of the two groupings, and their relative strength is likely to increase after Mao's death. Hua Kuo-feng, who was appointed Premier after Chou's death, presumably at Mao's initiative and in place of the now disgraced Teng, is clearly a compromise choice; but his background suggests a tilt toward the moderate side.

In view of the recent and drastic nature of these shifts, further unexpected developments could obviously occur before Mao's death, and even more so afterward. But in the absence of major intrusions from the outside, of which the most serious would be a Soviet attack, a resurgence of the radicals would reverse the net trend since the end of the Cultural Revolution, and still more since the fall of Lin Piao, toward ascendancy on the part of the moderates. The People's Liberation Army, although politically divided to some extent, tends to side with the moderates as long as its interests receive reasonable consideration from them.

The most plausible outlook for the succession to Mao is probably a period of some uncertainty and tension, from which will emerge a leadership that is more truly "collective" if only by virtue of Mao's absence, although there may very well be some interesting personnel changes. Such a leadership can reasonably be expected to be dominated—although not fully controlled—by moderate elements generally cooperating with the military, while the radicals will be allowed a representation and role that are more than token but less significant than at present.

The Outlook for Chinese Politics and Foreign Policy

After Mao's death, Chinese ideology and propaganda are likely to retain a strong Maoist coloration, if only because there is no available alternative. The real trend in politics and policymaking, however, is likely to be in directions that are not thought of as typically Maoist, although younger elements may from time to time attempt to regenerate revolutionary momentum along the lines laid down by Mao. China's external environment and domestic needs will not permit much more experimentation of the Maoist variety, and clearly require the application of policies associated with the moderates: reasonable political stability, social control, economic development, steady if unspectacular military modernization, and avoidance of unnecessary external quarrels. As a matter of fact, if one ignores Chinese propaganda—usually the best thing to do with it—the actual policy record to date, except during the hectic periods of the Great Leap Forward and the Cultural Revolution, approximate this model much more closely than is generally realized. Even a moderate Chinese leadership might continue to support "people's wars" in Asia and elsewhere in the Third World, either as a matter of choice or simply in fulfillment of previous commitments.

In foreign affairs, the probable trend toward pragmatism is likely to be accompanied by the persistence of a proud and sensitive nationalism, although perhaps less self-centered and less strident than in the past. Regardless of current issues, resentment of historic and recent Russian treatment of China will remain keen. The image of a Soviet threat may also be cultivated, with or without foundation, in order to promote leadership cohesion and popular obedience.

If the radicals, contrary to the future just projected, should play a dominant role after Mao, one would expect to see greater domestic turmoil, a closer linkage between domestic politics and foreign policy, a more assertive foreign policy, a weakening of the Sino-American detente, and a more truculent attitude toward the Soviet Union.

It appears to be in the Soviet—as well as the American—interest that the moderates hold the upper hand in Peking, as in fact they are likely to do. There is little doubt that Moscow would be interested in an accommodation with an essentially moderate post-Mao leadership in Peking, much as it tried to reach an accommodation with Mao himself in 1965. The Chinese attitude is more uncertain.

War, Peace, or Neither?

The general tendency of outside observers seems to assume that no major Sino-Soviet war is likely, because the risks and other disincentives on both sides are so great. A similar assumption is that the alternative of protracted confrontation, short of war and roughly along present lines, is hard to imagine because of its drawbacks, real or fancied, for both sides. Hence this chain of reasoning leaves as the only foreseeable outcome some kind of Sino-Soviet detente or rapprochement, presumably after Mao's death; and the current situation is ambiguous enough so that some evidence (such as Peking's release of the Soviet helicopter crew) can, in fact, be cited in support of the argument.

But none of these assumptions rests on a solid foundation. All three of the basic alternatives remain open, and there is no convincing reason for strongly preferring one to another. The future of the Sino-Soviet relationship is, therefore, essentially unpredictable, because the variables are too numerous and uncertain to make meaningful prediction possible.

Serious as the disincentives to war may be for both sides, there are plenty of issues to fight over; nations have gone to war over far less. The motivation is particularly strong on the Soviet side, which might decide, more on an emotional than rational basis, that the Chinese menace will inevitably grow worse and should, therefore, be dealt with by means of a military attack as soon as feasible, and before the Sino-American detente has time to solidify. A similar possibility is Soviet military intervention in an internal political crisis in China, probably after Mao's death, perhaps in support of a more or less pro-Soviet faction.

A prolonged confrontation without major war, but punctuated by occasional border clashes, is also possible. There are analogies in the hostility between Greece and Turkey, Israel and the Arab states, and India and Pakistan. In these cases, confrontation has been constrained, although war has not always been prevented, by the policies of the major powers. In the case of the Soviet Union and China, there are at least two major external constraints: uncertainty regarding the American reaction, and the possibility of crossing the nuclear threshold. But these considerations do not appear to eliminate the possibility of a prolonged confrontation. The situation could remain roughly as it is now, with neither side willing to make sufficient concessions to produce a genuine relaxation of tensions, and the Soviet side never considering conditions quite right for launching an attack.

Similarly, a Sino-Soviet rapprochement is certainly also a possibility. Just as it is the Chinese side that seems to gain more, or suffer less, from the present state of confrontation, it is the Soviet side that might gain (or at least think that it might gain) more from either an escalation of the confrontation to the level of war or a de-escalation in the form of detente or rapprochement. The problem obviously is that, thus far, Moscow has been unable or unwilling to offer terms attractive enough to overcome Peking's more or less conscious preference for confrontation. But a shift in the required direction on either side could produce a significant improvement in Sino-Soviet relations.

6

The Middle-Term Future:
The Successor Leaderships

Most of what was said in the preceding chapter about Sino-Soviet relations in the immediate aftermath of the departure of Brezhnev and Mao, including the wide range of developments that seem possible, will presumably continue to be applicable in the period after the two successor leaderships have become established. It may be helpful, however, to discuss these possible trends in greater detail, even though the analysis must inevitably be largely speculative.

In spite of repeated Soviet charges that China is aggressive, there is no evidence—and no plausible basis for believing—that China is likely to initiate a major military action against the Soviet Union. The military disincentives to such action would more than outweigh any possible or assumed political advantages, such as a unifying effect on the country at a time when tendencies toward disunity were appearing. Notwithstanding the impression conveyed by some of their bombastic propaganda, the Chinese are neither madmen nor suicidally inclined, and they are aware of the Soviet Union's military superiority. The only reasonable assumption, then, is that if war occurs it will be started by the Soviet side.

The first type of possible Soviet military action against China is what could be called political intervention, or in other words, the use of armed force with the aim of bringing about a political leadership and line favorable to Soviet interests. Given China's formidable powers of resistance, a Soviet offensive against an apparently united and hostile

Chinese regime, under some such pretext as the socalled Brezhnev Doctrine, appears very improbable if the object is the political purpose just mentioned. Political intervention would make sense only if significant "healthy forces" should materialize more or less spontaneously and ask for Soviet support. The "healthy forces" would presumably have to have a reasonable chance of winning the struggle against their domestic opponents even without Soviet support, or else they would appear simply as Soviet satellites in the event of success. Soviet political intervention would probably have to be richly rewarded by the new Chinese regime that had benefited from it, perhaps with a sphere of influence north of the Great Wall. Soviet military operations might be confined to that region, or they might include an armored thrust toward Peking from the Sino-Mongolian border.

Another conceivable type of politically motivated Soviet military action would be an ultimatum to Peking to take some particular step or face a Soviet attack, probably of an unspecified nature. Such an ultimatum would presumably be credible only if Peking were politically divided and internationally isolated; and even then it might very well be rejected. Other possible Soviet military actions would not be mainly political in motivation, in the sense that they would be based on the assumption of more or less incurable Chinese hostility to the Soviet Union, and would be designed to enhance Soviet security or promote some other Soviet interest regardless of the political impact on Peking. In reality, any sort of Soviet military action against China is likely to be politically counterproductive.

The most modest type of purely military action against China would probably be an occupation with conventional forces of some relatively small but strategic border areas, such as the Ili region in western Sinkiang or the Manchurian salient opposite Khabarovsk. From a military point of view, an operation of this kind would make sense and would probably be successful; but the consequences would almost certainly be serious unless China were already in a state of political dissolution. At a minimum, Peking would denounce the Soviet action with all its formidable propaganda and diplomatic resources, and thereby create a very embarrassing situation for Moscow that could seriously harm its international standing, especially in Asia. At the worst, Peking might launch—in addition to its political response—a retaliatory military action against vulnerable areas of Soviet Asia, including the Trans-Siberian Railway, in spite of its overall strategic inferiority. From such beginnings, the conflict could obviously escalate to the level of a major war.

Next on an ascending ladder of possible Soviet military moves would probably be a "surgical strike" against China's nuclear facilities (including missile sites), something for which the use of nuclear weapons would almost certainly be necessary. The risks of such a step would be very serious. There would be, in the first place, the same political and possible military consequences that would follow seizure of a limited border area, even if the strike were totally successful. But it probably would not be. Some combination of dispersal, concealment, hardening, and advance warning would probably enable a substantial fraction of Peking's nuclear missile force to be launched on warning and/or survive the Soviet attack, and strike back with unacceptable damage to important targets in the Soviet Union.

A more ambitious move would be an attempted Soviet occupation of some substantial region of China north of the Great Wall, such as Manchuria, Inner Mongolia, or Sinkiang, whether or not this was intended as a first step toward annexation or its transformation into a satellite area. Each of these would present a different combination of problems and possible gains. Because of its remoteness from China proper, Sinkiang would probably be the easiest and most tempting target, but its occupation by Soviet forces would probably yield the least losses to China and the least gains to the Soviet Union. Inner Mongolia is highly vulnerable to the powerful Soviet strike forces based in the Mongolian People's Republic, and is strategically very sensitive on account of its proximity to Peking; but in other respects (for example, economic) its importance is not very great. Manchuria is obviously less remote than Sinkiang, but more so than Inner Mongolia; it is of great economic importance, densely populated, and defended by roughly half a million Chinese soldiers. Regardless of which area, or which combination of areas, was selected as the target of a Soviet invasion, the political and military consequences would effectively be those of a general war between the Soviet Union and China, including some sort of Chinese retaliation against Soviet Asia, except that the war might be fought without the use of nuclear weapons.

A Sino-Soviet nuclear exchange, whether or not accompanied by a major conventional war, would of course create a greater risk of general war than any of the other possibilities. Indeed, it could be argued that the Soviet Union would probably not use nuclear weapons against countervalue (civilian) targets in China unless it were prepared for a possible nuclear war with the United States, and perhaps even unless it were prepared to launch such a war.

It is clear that at any level, the political costs and military risks of a Soviet attack on China are very high. This fact, and the probability that the situation is perceived similarly by a majority of the Soviet leadership, undoubtedly account largely for the fact that no such attack has occurred. By the same token, the probabilities are against any attack in the future. On the other hand, the possibility cannot be ruled out. Many of the wars of the 20th century appeared "unthinkable" almost until the moment of their outbreak.

Requirements for Detente

The probable minimum requirements for a Sino-Soviet detente in the strict sense of a relaxation of tensions can be simply stated. They include a significant and favorable alteration of the perception on each side of the other as a military and political threat. How could this be achieved?

In the first place, it would require a reduction of tension along the border. With or without formal agreement on the alignment of the boundary itself, each side—and the Soviet Union in particular—would have significantly to reduce its military presence along the border. This would probably have to be done simultaneously by both sides and on the basis of some kind of understanding, tacit or explicit.

On the political front, two things appear necessary. One is a more or less complete cessation of propaganda polemics on both sides, since such polemics now feed the atmosphere of mutual hostility that they also reflect. The other is a mitigation of the acute political rivalry and hostility in, and with respect to, third areas that now characterize the Sino-Soviet relationship. This would probably require, at a minimum, suspension of the Soviet campaign for "collective security" in Asia and the Chinese campaign to get other countries to subscribe to the "antihegemony" principle.

A Rapprochement Scenario

There are, of course, possible political relationships between the Soviet Union and China that are considerably closer than the rather modest one just outlined. The closest would be a full-fledged rapprochement that would restore something like the relatively cooperative relationship of the early 1950s. It would presumably contain four main components: ideology, interparty relations, interstate relations, and policy toward third countries.

Under current and probable future conditions, a rapprochement in the ideological field, given Chinese sensitivity on this subject (and even if the "thought" of Mao-Tse-tung were given less emphasis in China itself), would probably have to include some sort of Soviet recognition of Mao's "creative contribution" to the "treasury of Marxism-Leninism." This recognition would probably be much easier on the Soviet side if Mao were dead, and it would probably also require the prior passing from the scene of Mikhail Suslov, the principal Soviet leader who appears to care genuinely about ideology for its own sake. Each side would, of course, have to stop attacking the other's ideological positions and domestic political system in its propaganda.

In the field of interparty relations, which is widely but incorrectly regarded by non-Communists as being the same thing as ideology, a rapprochement would presumably begin with each side sending delegations to the other's Party congresses. On the Chinese side, no foreign delegations, Soviet or otherwise, have been invited to a Party congress since 1956; while on the Soviet side, foreign delegations have always been invited, but the last invitation extended to a Chinese delegation (in 1966) was refused. Beyond that, the Chinese Communist Party could agree to participate in international meetings of Communist Parties convened by Moscow, the last of which met in 1969 (without Chinese participation, of course).

In the field of interstate relations, the main elements would be a reduction, if not an elimination, of the current military confrontation, a boundary settlement, possibly a nonaggression pact and a renewal of the Sino-Soviet alliance (which expires in 1980), an increase in trade and technological exchanges, and a resumption of Soviet economic and military aid to China.

As for policy toward third countries, each side would have to indicate convincingly to the other its willingness to subordinate detente with the United States to the interests of its new relationship with the other, although not necessarily to the point of abandoning detente with the United States. Beyond that, and also the abandonment of "collective security" and "antihegemony" already referred to, there would have to be not only a cessation of acute hostility and rivalry, but also a considerable parallelism and probably even some active cooperation with respect to policy toward important third countries such as Japan. Moscow would have to reduce the level of its activity in Asia, and Peking would have to do the same in Europe.

A Possible Accommodation

To be meaningful, an improvement in Sino-Soviet relations would probably have to go beyond the minimum requirements for detente. But realistically speaking, it almost certainly could not go so far as the theoretical rapprochement just outlined; too much bad blood has arisen between Peking and Moscow in the last two decades for that.

A reasonable scenario for Sino-Soviet accommodation that might prove workable and might actually occur after the passing of Mao, Brezhnev, and Suslov from the scene would be roughly as follows.

There would be a substantial, although not necessarily total, cessation of polemics. In the ideological field, there would be a tacit agreement to live and let live, an arrangement that would probably intensify the already impressive tendencies toward pluralism or "polycentrism" in the Communist world. In other words, each side would refrain from either endorsing or attacking the other's ideological "line."

In the field of interparty relations, a limited restoration might well occur. That is to say, the Chinese could resume the practice of sending delegations to Soviet Party congresses, whether or not they again began to invite foreign (including Soviet) delegations to their own congresses. Peking would, however, probably continue to refrain from sending delegations to international conferences of Communist Parties sponsored by Moscow. This combination of policies would be what the Vietnamese and North Koreans have followed in recent years.

In the field of interstate relations, a reasonable combination of steps would involve a reduction of the military confrontation to a mutually tolerable level, a compromise boundary agreement, some increase in economic relations, but no resumption of Soviet aid to China.

As for third country policies, there might be a considerable reduction of general rivalry and hostility combined with continuing competitive policies toward critical countries such as the United States and Japan, but an absence of positive cooperation everywhere.

7

Aspects and Limits
of a Possible
Sino-Soviet Reconciliation

A full-fledged Sino-Soviet rapprochement or reconciliation is not likely. Such a development would have to take account of many difficult problems—more than those who predict its occurrence generally allow for—over and above the obvious and important obstacles created by emotional attitudes on both sides. This chapter tries to indicate some of the complications that might accompany, or prevent, a Sino-Soviet reconciliation.

Ideological Factors

Whether or not there are really "irreconcilable differences of principle" between the two parties to the Sino-Soviet dispute, as Peking maintained in a statement issued on October 7, 1969, there is no doubt that ideology plays an important part in the dispute, and will continue to do so for at least as long as Mao and Suslov are alive. Peking claims to see the Soviet political system as thoroughly "revisionist," and, even bourgeois, mainly in the sense of being motivated by a network of material incentives. Since the onset of the Cultural Revolution, on the other hand, Moscow has insisted that China is run by a coalition of Maoist radicals, military leaders, and bureaucrats, whose aims and methods have nothing in common with Marxism-Leninism. The Soviet side appears to be especially troubled—in part because of their possible exemplary effect on Soviet politics—by the weakening of the Communist Party apparatus, the enhanced political role of the military, and the relative freedom for public discussion of political issues that have characterized Chinese politics since about 1967. Each side appears to believe that the other is no longer "Socialist" (that is, Communist); and although both perceptions are consciously exaggerated for propaganda purposes, each is genuine to a high degree.

Apart from the two domestic systems, there are important differences of world outlook that have ideological overtones. The main divergence is not—or at least is no longer—over the proper attitude toward "imperialism," since the behavior of the two parties on this score is about equally opportunistic. Rather it is over the correct view of the Third World, with which China claims to identify itself and which it considers to be the "main force in the struggle against imperialism" (as Teng Hsiao-p'ing put it in a speech of April 1975) in a way that the Soviet Union cannot and will not do.

Unless and until the political influence of Maoism declines considerably, which is something that is not likely to happen in the near future, there appear to be only two ways out of this dilemma. One is Soviet acceptance of Maoism as a genuine and legitimate variant of Marxism-Leninism that is valid at least for China. The other is for the two parties to agree to differ, and thereafter to refrain from ideological polemics. Of these two outlooks, the latter seems less likely; but neither is a practical possibility at present.

Interparty Relations

In July 1963, delegations representing the Central Committees of the two parties and led by Suslov and Teng Hsiao-p'ing held acrimonious and unsuccessful talks in an alleged effort to resolve the differences between them. Although it was stated at the time, probably without much optimism, that further discussions would be held, none have been scheduled to date. This would be a logical and perhaps even an indispensable way to initiate a rapprochement in the field of interparty relations. Put differently, as long as such discussions are out of the question, as they appear to be at present, a restoration of interparty relations also appears impossible.

Probably of less substantive importance, but of considerable symbolic significance nonetheless, is the question of possible attendance by Chinese delegations at Soviet Party congresses and at international meetings of Communist Parties sponsored by Moscow. Conceivably this could happen even if the Chinese continued to keep their Party congresses closed to foreign observers. As in the case of the Central Committee talks, such attendance by Chinese delegations seems out of the question at present; and as long as that situation continues, there can be no full restoration of interparty relations between the Soviet Union and China.

Regardless of its likelihood, such a development would create serious problems for a number of Communist Parties which have benefited from the Sino-Soviet dispute through the increased autonomy it made possible. They would probably see in a restoration of Sino-Soviet interparty relations, especially if it occurred in the context of a trend toward a more or less full rapprochement, the threat of a revival of something like the old Comintern, this time under the joint leadership of Moscow and Peking.

The Border

The Sino-Soviet border dispute, and the military confrontation in the border region, have assumed so central a position in the Sino-Soviet controversy that a reconciliation is virtually unthinkable without a settlement of this issue at an early stage. There would have to be a ceasefire agreement, and some sort of force reduction along the border, in order to erase Peking's perception of the Soviet Union as a bully and a threat. There would have to be compromises on the areas in dispute, and some sort of new boundary agreement. A nonaggression pact as proposed by Moscow, however, and an acknowledgment that the old treaties were "unequal" as formerly demanded by Peking, would probably not be necessary. As one aid to terminating the atmosphere of tension that now prevails along the border, each side would have to stop trying to subvert the ethnic minorities on the other side. A settlement along these lines is neither impossible nor inevitable; but it is difficult, given the suspicion and resentment on both sides.

Military Relations

If there is a border settlement, it is possible that Sino-Soviet military relations will take on some sort of positive form. This possibility will presumably be enhanced if China fails in its recent behind-the-scenes efforts to buy advanced conventional weapon systems from private American producers.

The main possible elements of an improved Sino-Soviet military relationship would include sales of Soviet spare parts and new weapon systems, exchanges of information on matters of common professional interest between the two high commands, and a renewal of the Sino-Soviet alliance (in 1980). An improvement of this kind appears both less probable and less necessary to a general rapprochement than a settlement of the border dispute.

Economic Relations

Neither party to the Sino-Soviet dispute has any great need of the other as a trading partner, and economic affairs occupy only a minor position among the considerations that could promote rapprochement. The main factor of this kind would be a renewal of Soviet willingness— which was at least pretended in the early 1950s—to promote China's industrialization and general economic development through the extension of credits and technical assistance. Both the basic Soviet attitude toward China and the Maoist emphasis on economic "self-reliance"— which, to be sure, is honored more in theory than in practice—make such a development one of the least likely aspects of a Sino-Soviet rapprochement.

Politics and Diplomacy

The fundamental requirement for an improvement of political relations between Moscow and Peking is a substantial reduction of the mutual sense of threat and rivalry. Any progress in this respect must come mainly in the military field and in policy with respect to third countries. The first step might well be a shared sense of the futility of the current confrontation strong enough to overcome the present reluctance to make concessions sufficient to bring it to an end. Diminution of the current tendency to treat the other side as a demon figure for purposes of domestic and foreign propaganda would also be a great help.

Improvement along these lines also has certain internal political prerequisites. In the short and medium terms, the Soviet Union would have to maintain something like its current political stability. China, in turn, would have to attain a higher degree of political stability than it now has and, in order to establish respectability in Soviet eyes, would probably have to restore the Communist Party apparatus to the obviously controlling position in the political system that it held before the

Cultural Revolution. In the long run, some significant development in the direction of a plural or "open" society, whose operation does not require the maintenance of a foreign demon image for purposes of political mobilization, will probably be necessary if the poisonous propaganda of each side against the other is to be reduced to mutually tolerable levels. It is obvious that there has been almost no movement in this direction on either side to date.

Policy Toward Third Areas

A Sino-Soviet rapprochement would almost certainly require that the Soviet Union abandon its current afforts to cultivate the general impression that it has some sort of Taiwan card to play—in other words, that it might establish some sort of relationship with the Republic of China as a means, among other things, of obstructing the union of Taiwan with the mainland. The sensitivity of this issue in Peking goes far beyond any actual gestures the Soviet Union has so far made in the direction of Taiwan. These have been rather minor, but they have been just sufficient to create the impression alluded to.

Just as the United States has figured prominently, although not always consciously, in the Sino-Soviet dispute, so it would probably figure in a Sino-Soviet rapprochement. Each side could be expected to downgrade somewhat the importance it currently attaches to detente with the United States, without necessarily abandoning the detente. It is improbable, however, that Moscow and Peking would, or indeed could, go so far as to restore the relative militant solidarity of the early 1950s in confronting the United States. Too much has changed in the international environment, and in Sino-Soviet relations, for that.

Japan is another important country that would almost certainly be involved in, and affected by, a Sino-Soviet rapprochement. As in the case of the United States, the situation of the early 1950s—in which Moscow and Peking in considerable measure concerted their hostile policies toward Japan—is unlikely to be restored. Nevertheless, Japanese interests would tend to be adversely affected by a Sino-Soviet rapprochement. This would be especially true if, as does not seem likely at present, Moscow and Peking agreed to support Kim Il-sung's efforts to take over South Korea. Even without that, Moscow and Peking would have to be concerned that a rapprochement between them might cause Japan to rearm on a massive scale, perhaps including nuclear weapons. Such an outcome would be worse from the point of view of both Communist powers than the obvious alternative, namely, a tightening of Japan's security ties with the United States. Given the problems just mentioned, a Sino-Soviet rapprochement would probably have to include some provision for coping with Japan; one approach would be to eliminate Japan as the adversary specified in the Sino-Soviet treaty of alliance, assuming that the latter is renewed in 1980.

A Sino-Soviet rapprochement would probably also have to include some understanding on a reduction of Soviet diplomatic and other activity in Asia, and of similar Chinese activity in Europe. Sino-Soviet rivalry in the Third World (apart from Asia) is almost equally sensitive, for ideological and other reasons, and a full-scale Sino-Soviet rapprochement would probably be impossible without some reduction of it. In particular, Peking would probably have to moderate, or even abandon, its claim to a special affinity with the Third World, and its assertions that its own experience in making revolution constitutes a uniquely valuable model for the Third World, except in the extremely unlikely event that the Soviet Union were willing to concede Peking's claims in this connection as part of the price of rapprochement.

8

Implications for the United States

The United States has always occupied a position of special importance with respect to the Sino-Soviet relationship, both in its own eyes and in those of the parties. It seems likely that this will continue to be true, regardless of whatever course the Sino-Soviet relationship actually follows.

American Policy and the Sino-Soviet Confrontation

At the time of the Sino-Soviet border crisis in 1969, the public American position was simply to express hope that there would be no war. So far as is known, no indication was given of any intent to give positive support to China as the weaker party essentially on the defensive. The crisis undoubtedly did intensify American efforts to improve relations with Peking. This was done, however, with no particular sense that it was possible to "exploit" the Sino-Soviet confrontation. On the contrary, repeated official statements have stressed that the policy of the United States is one of "equidistance" between the Soviet Union and China and noninterference in their relations with one another. This position, which has been fairly close to the actual policy, has apparently reflected a sense that the United States was unable to do very much directly about the confrontation, and an unwillingness either to endanger the American detente with the Soviet Union or to risk precipitating further Soviet pressures on China by moving too far and too fast to help strengthen Peking's hand in coping with its Soviet problem.

Chinese sources have claimed that, in 1974, the United States gave Peking strategic warning of apparently threatening Soviet military movements near the Chinese border. There has been no confirmation of this report from the American side. In any event, it is certain that the United States government has neither considered giving China a military guarantee of any kind, nor have we been asked to do so. Peking has privately approached some major American manufacturers of advanced conventional weapon systems, but the US government has so far not reached a decision to permit such sales. The question is very sensitive for several reasons, including both American and Chinese domestic politics and the possible Soviet response.

The United States and a Sino-Soviet War

American policymakers have looked with strong disfavor on the prospect of a Sino-Soviet war, and with good reason. Such a war, if it were fought on a more than localized scale, would probably result in some sort of defeat for China; and this would have highly destabilizing effects on its already somewhat shaky political system. It is worth remembering, as most Chinese do, that when in the past China was disunited, weak, or defeated in war, it often became the object of conflicting pressures and rivalries on the part of the great powers. In fact, China's weakness has been the principal cause of war in the Far East since the late 19th century. If China were to fall into such a condition again as a result of defeat at the hands of the Soviet Union, the outcome would be a serious blow to the multilateral balance of power in the Far East that the United States has been trying to promote since about 1969. Furthermore, the United States would probably find itself in the embarrassing position of being both unable and unwilling to do anything timely and effective to prevent a Chinese defeat at the hands of the Soviet Union; and American "credibility" would be further weakened.

It is clearly in the American interest, then, that a Sino-Soviet war be avoided. To date, the main American contribution to preventing such a war has been some verbal tut-tutting to the Soviet Union (at the 1972 Moscow summit conference, reportedly), and the establishment of a relationship with China calculated to constrain Moscow's behavior by creating a significant uncertainty on its part as to what the American response to a Soviet attack on China would be. Even though there has obviously been no such attack to date, it can be argued that existing American policy is inadequate to its purposes and needs strengthening. Some possible steps in this direction are suggested in the last section of this chapter.

The United States and a Continuing Sino-Soviet Confrontation

Thus far, the United States can be considered to have benefited from the Sino-Soviet confrontation, without having caused it or having been able actively to exploit it. The United States has benefited mainly in that confrontation has greatly intensified the interest of both Moscow and Peking in seeking detente with the United States. This has fitted in very well with the purposes of American policymakers, even though one may legitimately doubt how beneficial detente with the Soviet Union and China has actually been to the United States.

Putting these doubts aside, if we assume that detente is in the American interest, a continuation of the Sino-Soviet confrontation is presumably also in the American interest. But it is at least equally clear that there is little if anything that the United States can do to promote a continuation of the confrontation, since it has been generated by factors on both sides that go far beyond their attitudes toward and relationships with the United States.

The United States and a Sino-Soviet Detente

It is hard to avoid the conclusion that just as a deterioration of the Sino-Soviet relationship in the direction of war would be adverse to American interests, so would movement in the opposite direction.

But how adverse? A Sino-Soviet detente would probably diminish the interest of each party in pursuing detente with the United States, but would not necessarily eliminate that interest. The Soviet-American detente and the Sino-American detente do not rest exclusively on the foundation of Sino-Soviet confrontation.

In the long run, the United States can learn to live with a Sino-Soviet detente and may have to do so. For reasons already suggested, a reduction of military tension between Moscow and Peking would be advantageous to the United States because of the resulting decline in the chances for a war that would be highly adverse to American interests. Similarly, the United States should have no serious problem, at least in the long run, with a reduction of ideological hostility and propaganda polemics between China and the Soviet Union. The real problem would begin, of course, if significant cooperation were to be achieved by the two Communist powers with respect to third areas, above all the United States itself, Japan, and Western Europe. As already suggested, however, this sort of cooperation is likely to prove one of the most difficult things to achieve even if Sino-Soviet relations take a definite turn for the better.

From an overall theoretical point of view, a Sino-Soviet detente might help to produce a reasonably close approximation of the five-sided international balance (consisting of the United States, the Soviet Union, China, Japan, and Western Europe) that American policy-makers have sometimes posited as the optimum scenario for international politics. Ideally, this kind of balance would presumably work best if no two of the actors were in a state of either acute conflict or close collaboration with each other. Two possible alternate models of international politics must be regarded with great suspicion on historical grounds: a confrontation between two rival coalitions, which produced World War I; and the concentration of clearly superior power and greater aggressiveness in the hands of a single power as compared with the others, which led to World War II.

The United States and a Sino-Soviet Reconciliation

If a Sino-Soviet detente would have some advantages, or at any rate consolations, for the United States, the same could not be said of a full-fledged Sino-Soviet rapprochement or reconciliation. Such a development, even if it stopped short of a complete restoration of the relationship of the early 1950s, could be a serious threat to American interests. Assuming, as seems plausible, that the two Communist regimes retained their current highly authoritarian character, they would still require the image of an external adversary. This would obviously be mainly the United States under the conditions of a Sino-Soviet rapprochement, which would by definition eliminate Moscow and Peking as demon figures to each other.

In the long run, of course, it is possible that—in parallel with this hypothetical rapprochement—the Soviet Union and China would become more nearly "open" societies. would cease to require an external demon figure, and would improve their relations with the United States on a genuine and lasting basis. But such a near-ideal situation seems too much even to hope for except in the long run, in which, as Keynes pointed out, we are all dead.

Meanwhile, what could the United States do, in a general way, to minimize the chances of a Sino-Soviet rapprochement? The answer seems to be, Not very much. In the past, the United States made its contribution, which was great although not quite decisive, to the emergence of the Sino-Soviet dispute largely unconsciously, simply by promoting its own interests as it saw them—by acting to keep Taiwan out of Communist hands, for example. This seems to be the best future plan as well: namely, to do what seems to be required by American interests, without worrying unduly about the effect on the Sino-Soviet relationship, many aspects of which are clearly beyond the power of the United States to influence directly.

Possible American Policy Initiatives

As long as the Sino-Soviet relationship continues to be essentially a confrontation, there is obviously some danger of war; and as already indicated, this would be adverse to American interests. What could the United States do to reduce the chances of a Sino-Soviet war? Since China is clearly the weaker party, a Sino-Soviet war would have to involve a Soviet attack of some sort on China, and an effective American policy would therefore have to include measures intended to strengthen China's position. As already suggested, explicit military guarantees appear to be out of the question. But there are things that could be done that fall short of that, and yet would go beyond present policy.

One would be the transfer, through governmental or private channels, or both, of advanced American conventional weapons systems. For all its obvious attractiveness as a partial equalizer of the Sino-Soviet military balance, such a program would be a very sensitive matter in the domestic politics and foreign relations of both China and the United States. Any transfer large enough to be helpful to China would enhance its capabilities not only against the Soviet Union, but ultimately against the United States and its Asian allies as well. The reaction on the part of the latter, and still more on the part of the Soviet Union, might be severe enough to affect adversely the interests of both China and the United States.

A less controversial move that would nevertheless be helpful to China would be an American commitment to provide Peking with advance strategic warning of any Soviet military moves, including maneuvers, that appeared to be threatening to China. Peking is developing its own satellite reconnaissance and radar network, but they are probably still inadequate to guarantee against surprise. For maximum effectiveness, such a commitment should be publicly announced. Moscow would obviously not be pleased; but since it has repeatedly denied any intent to attack China, it could not reasonably do much more than get irritated.

A more political, and probably more effective, step would be for the United States to announce publicly and authoritatively that in the event of a Soviet attack on China, it would regard the entire Soviet-American detente, not necessarily as dead, but as subject to complete re-examination. The probable results of this re-examination should not be announced, but should be left to Moscow's imagination. This should be a powerful disincentive to a Soviet attack on China so long as Moscow's interest in detente with the United States continues at anything like its present level.

American measures likely to discourage the opposite contingency, a Sino-Soviet rapprochement, are more difficult to devise. Probably the best single move of this kind would be a more careful cultivation of Japanese-American relations, so as to keep open, and conspicuously open, the possibility of a close working relationship in opposition to a Sino-Soviet rapprochement if one should materialize. This would mean more sensitive American attention than has been usual in the recent past to Japan's needs and reasonable expectations in successive situations. At present, this would mean full official cooperation with the Japanese investigation of the Lockheed scandal, and greater consideration for Japanese interests in economic matters (trade and investment policies) than has been shown in the recent past, particularly by the Nixon Administration. In addition, the United States should not reach a decision to withdraw its remaining troops from South Korea without carefully considering the possibly adverse impact of such a move on Japan's sense of security. If Japanese political pressures for a revision of the security treaty with the United States or for closing down American bases in Japan and Okinawa become significant, the United States would probably do better to comply in the hope of preserving a more important asset, its underlying friendship with Japan.

In addition, regardless of the future of the Sino-Soviet relationship, if the United States is to have any effective influence on that relationship and on the general future of Asia, it must maintain an active political interest and a significant military presence in the region. In the military context, this would include the maintenance of bases and forces in South Korea, Japan, and the Philippines to the extent that local political conditions permit, plus Guam and the northern Marianas, as well as seaborne forces in the western Pacific. Above all, the United States must convey, not merely through its physical capabilities but by its political behavior, that it is a power that knows its interests and is determined to promote them, in so far as possible without infringing on the legitimate interests of others. An image of this kind is not the one that the United States has projected in recent years.

A Note on Sources

The main sources for this study, as for any serious study of Sino-Soviet relations, are the policy statements, press, radio, and periodical literature of the two sides, which not only give their political and propaganda positions, but also—although not completely—the record of their actual behavior toward each other. The radio output, and to a much more limited extent the press, on each side can be followed in the relevant series of *Foreign Radio Broadcasts* published by the Foreign Broadcast Information Service (Washington). On the Soviet side, see also the *Current Digest of the Soviet Press* (New York). On the Chinese side, see the various series of translations published by the American Consulate General, Hong Kong, especially *Survey of the People's Republic of China Press* (formerly *Survey of the China Mainland Press*). For a convenient sampling on the Chinese side, see *Peking Review*; on the Soviet side, see *International Affairs, New Times,* and *Far Eastern Affairs.*

No serious student should neglect the best of the Western press as a source and commentary on the basic record of the two Communist powers. The *New York Times* and *Washington Post* (especially the weekly columns of Victor Zorza) deserve particular attention in this respect.

The official Soviet view of an important slice of the history of Sino-Soviet relations is presented in O. B. Borisov (pseud.) and B. T. Koloskov (pseud.), *Soviet-Chinese Relations, 1945-1970,* edited by Vladimir Petrov, Indiana University Press, 1975. There is no comparable work from the Chinese side, although Peking's major polemics of the late Khrushchev period are conveniently collected in *The Polemic on the General Line of the International Communist Movement,* Foreign Languages Press, 1965.

The classic study of the origins of the Sino-Soviet dispute is Donald S. Zagoria, *The Sino-Soviet Conflict, 1956-1961,* Princeton University Press, 1962. Other excellent studies of the preconfrontation phase are William E. Griffith, *Albania and the Sino-Soviet Rift,* M.I.T. Press, 1963; William E. Griffith, *The Sino-Soviet Rift,* M.I.T. Press, 1964; William E. Griffith, *Sino-Soviet Relations, 1964-1965,* M.I.T. Press, 1967; John Gittings, ed., *Survey of the Sino-Soviet Dispute: A Commentary and Extracts from the Recent Polemics, 1963-1967,* Oxford University Press, 1968; Raymond L. Garthoff, ed., *Sino-Soviet Military Relations,* Praeger, 1966; and Morton H. Halperin, ed., *Sino-Soviet Relations and Arms Control,* M.I.T. Press, 1967.

Valuable sources bearing on the confrontation phase of Sino-Soviet relations are Tai Sung An, *The Sino-Soviet Territorial Dispute,* Westminster Press, 1973; Dennis J. Doolin, ed., *Territorial Claims in the Sino-Soviet Conflict: Documents and Analysis,* Hoover Institution, 1965; Harrison E. Salisbury, *War Between Russia and China,* Bantam, 1970; Morris Rothenberg, *Soviet Perceptions of the Chinese Succession,* University of Miami Center for Advanced International Studies, no date (1975?); Thomas W. Robinson, "The Sino-Soviet Border Dispute: Background, Development, and the March 1969 Clashes," *American Political Science Review,* vol. 66, no. 4 (December 1972), pp. 1175-1202; "The Border Issue: China and the Soviet Union, March-October 1969," *Studies in Comparative Communism,* vol. 2, nos. 3-4 (July-October 1969), pp. 130-382; Harold C. Hinton, "Sino-Soviet Relations in the Brezhnev Era," *Current History,* vol. 61, no. 361 (September 1971), pp. 135-141, 181; Harold C. Hinton, "Conflict on the Ussuri: A Clash of Nationalisms," *Problems of Communism,* vol. 20, nos. 1-2 (January-April 1971), pp. 45-59; Harold C. Hinton, *The Bear at the Gate: Chinese Policymaking under Soviet Pressure,* American Enterprise Institute and Hoover Institution, 1971; and Harold C. Hinton, "The United States and the Sino-Soviet Confrontation," *Orbis,* vol. 19, no. 1 (Spring 1975), pp. 25-46. In addition, mention should be made of the important papers on the Sino-Soviet dispute (as well as many other topics) written by Christian Duevel for Radio Liberty (in *Radio Liberty Dispatches*) and by Joseph C. Kun for Radio Free Europe (in *Radio Free Europe Research Papers*) and Radio Libetry.

National Strategy Information Center, Inc.

STRATEGY PAPERS
Edited by Frank N. Trager and William Henderson
With the assistance of Dorothy E. Nicolosi

The Sino-Soviet Confrontation: Implications for the Future by Harold C. Hinton, September 1976

Food, Foreign Policy, and Raw Materials Cartels by William Schneider, February 1976

Strategic Weapons: An Introduction by Norman Polmar, October 1975

Soviet Sources of Military Doctrine and Strategy by William F. Scott, July 1975

Detente: Promises and Pitfalls by Gerald L. Steibel, March 1975

Oil, Politics, and Sea Power: The Indian Ocean Vortex by Ian W. A. C. Adie, December 1974

The Soviet Presence in Latin America by James D. Theberge, June 1974

The Horn of Africa by J. Bowyer Bell, Jr., December 1973

Research and Development and the Prospects for International Security by Frederick Seitz and Rodney W. Nichols, December 1973

Raw Material Supply in a Multipolar World by Yuan-li Wu. October 1973

The People's Liberation Army: Communist China's Armed Forces by Angus M. Fraser, August 1973 (Out of print)

Nuclear Weapons and the Atlantic Alliance by Wynfred Joshua, May 1973

How to Think About Arms Control and Disarmament by James E. Dougherty, May 1973

The Military Indoctrination of Soviet Youth by Leon Goure, January 1973 (Out of print)

The Asian Alliance: Japan and United States Policy by Franz Michael and Gaston J. Sigur, October 1972

Iran, The Arabian Peninsula, and the Indian Ocean by R. M. Burrell and Alvin J. Cottrell, September 1972 (Out of print)

Soviet Naval Power: Challenge for the 1970s by Norman Polmar, April 1972. Revised edition, September 1974

How Can We Negotiate with the Communists? by Gerald L. Steibel, March 1972 (Out of print)

Soviet Political Warfare Techniques, Espionage and Propaganda in the 1970s by Lyman B. Kirkpatrick, Jr., and Howland H. Sargeant, January 1972

The Soviet Presence in the Eastern Mediterranean by Lawrence L. Whetten, September 1971

The Military Unbalance
   Is the U.S. Becoming a Second Class Power? June 1971 (Out of print)

The Future of South Vietnam by Brigadier F. P. Serong, February 1971 (Out of print)

Strategy and National Interests: Reflections for the Future by Bernard Brodie, January 1971 (Out of print)

The Mekong River: A Challenge in Peaceful Development for Southeast Asia by Eugene R. Black, December 1970 (Out of print)

Problems of Strategy in the Pacific and Indian Oceans by George G. Thomson, October 1970

Soviet Penetration into the Middle East by Wynfred Joshua, July 1970. Revised edition, October 1971 (Out of print)

Australian Security Policies and Problems by Justus M. van der Kroef, May 1970 (Out of print)

Detente: Dilemma or Disaster? by Gerald L. Steibel, July 1969 (Out of print)

The Prudent Case for Safeguard by William R. Kintner, June 1969 (Out of print)

AGENDA PAPERS
Edited by Frank N. Trager and William Henderson
With the assistance of Dorothy E. Nicolosi

Toward a New Defense for NATO, The Case for Tactical Nuclear Weapons, July 1976

Seven Tracks to Peace in the Middle East by Frank R. Barnett, April 1975

Arms Treaties with Moscow: Unequal Terms Unevenly Applied? by Donald G. Brennan, April 1975

Toward a US Energy Policy by Klaus Knorr, March 1975

Can We Avert Economic Warfare in Raw Materials? US Agriculture as a Blue Chip by William Schneider, July 1974

OTHER PUBLICATIONS

Alternatives to Detente by Frank R. Barnett, July 1976

Arms, Men, and Military Budgets, Issues for Fiscal Year 1977 edited by William Schneider, Jr., and Francis P. Hoeber, May 1976

Indian Ocean Naval Limitations, Regional Issues and Global Implications by Alvin J. Cottrell and Walter F. Hahn, April 1976

71

NATIONAL STRATEGY INFORMATION CENTER, INC.

OFFICERS

FRANK R. BARNETT*
President
DR. FRANK N. TRAGER
Director of Studies
Professor of
International Affairs,
Director, National Security
Program
New York University
ROBERT G. BURKE*
Secretary, Treasurer, and
General Counsel
Burke and Cerutti
New York, New York
*Also Directors

PAUL E. FEFFER*
International Vice President
President
Feffer & Simons, Inc.
New York, New York
JOHN G. McKAY, JR.*
Vice President
Bradford, Williams, McKay,
Kimbrell, Hamann & Jennings, P.A.
Miami, Florida
DOROTHY E. NICOLOSI
Assistant Secretary,
Assistant Treasurer, and
Executive Administrator

DIRECTORS

KARL R. BENDETSEN
Director and Retired Chairman
Champion International Corporation
D. TENNANT BRYAN
Chairman of the Board
Media General, Inc.
RICHARD C. HAM
Attorney at Law
San Francisco, California
MORRIS I. LEIBMAN
Sidley & Austin
Chicago, Illinois
REAR ADMIRAL WILLIAM C.
   MOTT, USN (Ret.)
Executive Vice President
U. S. Independent Telephone
   Association
Washington, D. C.
JOHN C. NEFF
New York, New York

ROBERT H. PARSLEY
Butler, Binion, Rice, Cook and Knapp
Houston, Texas
DR. EUGENE V. ROSTOW
Professor of Law
Yale University Law School
New Haven, Connecticut
HON. FRANK SHAKESPEARE
President
RKO General, Inc.
JAMES L. WINOKUR
Chairman of the Board
Air Tool Parts and Service Company
MAJOR GENERAL RICHARD
   A. YUDKIN, USAF (Ret.)
Senior Vice President
Owens-Corning Fiberglas Corporation
Toledo, Ohio

ADVISORY COUNCIL

JOSEPH COORS
Executive Vice President
Adolph Coors Company
HON. HENRY H. FOWLER
Goldman, Sachs & Co.
JOHN W. HANES, JR.
Wertheim & Co.
DILLARD MUNFORD
President
Munford, Inc.

HON. ADOLPH W. SCHMIDT
Former Ambassador to Canada
DR. FREDERICK SEITZ
President
Rockefeller University
JAMES G. SHIELDS, JR.
Executive Vice President
Crocker National Corp.
JOHN A. SUTRO
Pillsbury, Madison & Sutro

STAFF

O. E. PACE
HUGH McGOWAN
Assistants to the President

Washington Associate
DR. ROY GODSON
Assistant Professor of Government
Director, International Labor
   Program
Georgetown University